Facilitating
Authentic
Learning

GRADES 6–12

For my first teachers, Nelson and Patricia Richter and Heather Kiley, and for John, Harry, and Molly, who remind me every day why I do the work I do.

Facilitating Authentic Learning

GRADES 6–12

A Framework for
Student-Driven
Instruction

Laura R. Thomas

Foreword by Jill Davidson

CORWIN
A SAGE Company

CORWIN
A SAGE Company

FOR INFORMATION:

Corwin

A SAGE Company

2455 Teller Road

Thousand Oaks, California 91320

(800) 233-9936

www.corwin.com

SAGE Publications Ltd.

1 Oliver's Yard

55 City Road

London EC1Y 1SP

United Kingdom

SAGE Publications India Pvt. Ltd.

B 1/I 1 Mohan Cooperative Industrial Area

Mathura Road, New Delhi 110 044

India

SAGE Publications Asia-Pacific Pte. Ltd.

3 Church Street

#10-04 Samsung Hub

Singapore 049483

Acquisitions Editor: Robin Najar

Editorial Assistant: Lisa Whitney

Production Editor: Cassandra Margaret Seibel

Copy Editor: Paula L. Fleming

Typesetter: C&M Digitals (P) Ltd.

Proofreader: Caryne Brown

Indexer: Jean Casalegno

Cover Designer: Bryan Fishman

Permissions Editor: Adele Hutchinson

Printed in the United States of America

Library of Congress Cataloging-in-Publication Data

Thomas, Laura R. author.

Facilitating authentic learning, grades 6 - 12 : a framework for student-driven instruction / Laura R. Thomas.

pages cm
Includes bibliographical references and index.

ISBN 978-1-4522-1648-5 (pbk.)

1. Active learning. 2. Education, Secondary. I. Title.

LB1027.23.T54 2013
371.39—dc23   2012020441

This book is printed on acid-free paper.

MIX
Paper from
responsible sources
FSC
www.fsc.org   FSC® C014174

12 13 14 15 16 10 9 8 7 6 5 4 3 2 1

Contents

List of Figures and Boxes   vii

Foreword   ix
  Jill Davidson

Preface   xi

Acknowledgments   xiii

About the Author   xv

Introduction   1

Meet the Facilitators   4

1. **What Is Next Generation Instruction?**   17
   What Are the Purposes of Next Generation Instruction?   21

2. **Laying the Groundwork: Building a Collaborative Learning Community**   25
   Recognizing the Collaborative Learning Community   28
   Stages of Building and Maintaining a Collaborative
      Learning Community   30
   Creating the Collaborative Learning Community   32

3. **Aiming: Gaining Clarity**   48
   The Framework for Next Generation Instructional Facilitation   49

4. **Framing and Gaming**   56
   Framing   56
   Gaming   67

5. **Claiming and Exclaiming: Reflection**   77
   Claiming   77
   Exclaiming   94

6. Tips, Activities, and Tools for Next Generation Instruction:
    Gaming, Claiming, and Exclaiming   97
    Activities and Tools for Gaming, Claiming, and Exclaiming   99

7. Assessment   103

8. Conclusion   135

Appendix: Additional Resources   138

References   141

Index   143

List of Figures and Boxes

Box 1.1	A Note About Technology	20
Figure 1.1	Framework for Next Generation Instruction: Overview	24
Figure 2.1	Framework for Next Generation Instruction: Collaborative Learning Community	26
Figure 2.2	Zones of Relative Risk Taking	36
Figure 2.3	Different Students, Different Risk Zones	38
Box 2.1	Give to Get Instructions	41
Figure 2.4	Classroom Policies, Group Created	42
Figure 2.5	Base Teams Challenge	43
Figure 2.6	Academic Support	44
Box 3.1	Resources for Planning Instruction	49
Figure 3.1	Framework for Next Generation Instruction: Aiming	50
Figure 4.1	Framework for Next Generation Instruction: Framing	57
Box 4.1	Frontloading	58
Box 4.2	Great Aunt Mildred's U.S. Road Trip and Great Aunt Mildred's Space Shot	60
Box 4.3	Religion Poster	63
Box 4.4	Ford Motor Company Challenge	66
Figure 4.2	Framework for Next Generation Instruction: Gaming	68
Box 4.3	My Favorite Questions for Responding to (Student) Questions	74

Figure 5.1   Framework for Next Generation
Instruction: Claiming   78

Figure 5.2   Physical Science (Classical Mechanics)
Learning Level Data Table   80

Figure 5.3   Chemistry Learning Level Data Table   81

Figure 5.4   Biology Learning Level Data Table   82

Figure 5.5   Questions to Prompt Claiming (Reflection)   83

Box 5.1   Souhegan High School Mission
Statement and Souhegan Six—Souhegan
High School Behavioral Expectations   90

Figure 5.6–5.9 Reflection Rubrics   91–94

Figure 5.10   Framework for Next Generation
Instruction: Exclaiming   95

Figure 7.1   Example End-of-Day Sheet   109

Box 7.1   Setting Quality Criteria: A Procedure   110

Figure 7.2   Guidelines for Giving and Receiving Feedback   113

Figure 7.3   Example Leadership Checklist   114

Figure 7.4   Example Organization Checklist   116

Figure 7.5   Example Self-Direction Checklist   118

Figure 7.6   Example Collaboration Checklist   119

Figure 7.7   Example Checklist Rubric for Product Quality   121

Figure 7.8   Example Challenge Feedback   122

Figure 7.9   Example Oral Communications Rubric   123

Figure 7.10   Example Effort and Participation Rubric   125

Figure 7.11   Example Science Progress Report   127

Figure 7.12   Great Aunt Mildred's Space Shot Rubric   128

Figure 7.13   Great Aunt Mildred's U.S. Tour Rubric   131

Figure 8.1   Framework for Next Generation
Instruction: Complete   136

Foreword

For more than a dozen years, I have worked on behalf of the Coalition of Essential Schools (CES), a national network of schools and support organizations focused on creating the best possible conditions for learning and achievement. CES has pitched a big tent that includes in-district public, charter, and independent schools that serve elementary, middle, and high school students in all parts of the United States and beyond. This broad array of schools demonstrates CES's precept that "no two schools are alike," and teachers in Essential schools represent the widest possible range of races, economic classes, cultures, linguistic backgrounds, regions, and sexual orientations. Yet within all of this diversity, effective CES educators are remarkably similar in the ways that they work with students to create collaborative classroom environments. CES educators facilitate learning, developing in their students habits of mind and heart that serve them well throughout their lives.

I count Laura Thomas as one of the masters of this way of teaching, and I am thrilled that she has so carefully, joyfully, and precisely brought to life the ways in which teachers can coach students to work with others, ask questions, try difficult things, and reach their fullest potential as learners who meet and exceed established standards of learning. Thomas puts her own experience as an educator, scholar, and parent to work in these pages. She draws from her own experiences, challenges, and insights to delineate a path to becoming an educator who facilitates understanding and skill building within a community of learners. Thomas also brings us into the classrooms of educators who have made the same passage, fusing a variety of experience with a solid theoretical framework and thereby creating an immediately practical, useful, and inspiring resource for educators at all points along the spectrum of experience.

Before I send you on your own journey through the pages of *Facilitating Authentic Learning: A Framework for Student-Driven Instruction*, I want to share a final appreciation. Thomas and the educators whose work she has researched and shares here insist that in classrooms where real, meaningful work gets done, failure is not only an option but an imperative—a required stop on the way to meaningful learning. The pressure is so very high for educators and students that we often forget to reflect on mistakes. We therefore miss the most potent and enduring kind of learning. Educators who have developed skills as facilitators both understand that mistakes can and will happen as students develop and know how to guide students to reflect on and learn from those mistakes.

This ability to resist the pressure to go for tidy, correct answers in favor of facilitating the messy business of real learning is a hallmark of effective and enduring educators. Thomas encourages educators to be brave and guides them through their own learning. She anticipates their challenges and gives them a generous tool kit to use as they become "Next Generation instructors"—a wonderfully apt description of teachers focused on the long-term success of their students.

Jill Davidson
Educators for Social Responsibility

Preface

This is the book I wish I'd had in 1993. As a young, energetic first-year teacher, facing my own class of teenagers (who were not noticeably younger than I), I wanted to be more than a Good Teacher. I wanted to be Amazing. Life Changing. I wanted to Shape Young Minds and Change Lives. The problem?

I hadn't the faintest idea how.

I'd graduated from an excellent preparation program, and I knew the ins and outs of policy, assessment, and curriculum design. I was fluent in a number of pedagogical theories, and I had my content down cold. What I didn't know was how to actually teach. Or, more specifically, how to teach beyond the way I had been taught. It took me only a week to realize that the tried-and-true methods had worked for me as a student because I was a traditional learner. I responded well to lecture, I liked taking notes, and writing—essays, papers, short-answer responses—was easy for me. Most of my students, however, were not like me. While some were willing to play what Rob Fried calls "the game of school" (Fried, 2005), the traditional "lecture and test" or read-the-chapter-and-answer-the-questions-at-the-end schtick wasn't really getting us anywhere.

So, like the good student I was, I hit the books. I revisited my Dewey. I rediscovered Sizer and Meier and Goodlad. Their words made sense: "Student as worker" and "habits of mind" all resonated with me in a deep and powerful way. What I lacked, however, was a way to turn those ideas into lesson plans I could use on Thursday. I had the textbook, of course, and a curriculum guide, but neither of those was any help.

I needed help.

Luckily, the education gods intervened, and I changed jobs quickly, moving into a school that had been awarded a large five-year grant to "innovate" (whatever we decided that meant), and the results saved my pedagogical soul. We joined the nascent Coalition of Essential Schools, and I was lucky enough to find myself surrounded by teachers and administrators who were engaged in the same struggle as I. We created one of the first Critical Friends Groups in the nation, allowing me to be part of a group of reflective practitioners in the formative years of my career. I wrote a Learn and Serve America grant and watched as my students deepened my understanding of service learning. I read and discussed more books and was allowed to attend more truly excellent institutes, conferences, and workshops in the next four years than most teachers attend in ten. I was encouraged to step beyond the curriculum guide, to take risks, and to fail brilliantly in service to our shared journey toward meaningful instruction.

Not only was this a seminal professional experience for me, but it laid the foundation for this book as it pushed me to look at my own experiences—both within and outside the field—to improve my practice. During my undergraduate years, I'd been fortunate to work for the American Youth Foundation (AYF) as part of summer camp staff in the dunes of Michigan and the mountains of New Hampshire. In the intervening years, they had refined their philosophy, a Framework for Facilitation, for use in their own work, and this was brought to my attention nearly 15 years later by Heather Kiley, director of Merrowvista (and—not incidentally—my sister). Learning about the Framework codified my own first introductions to experiential learning, my early teaching experiences, my graduate work at Antioch University–New England (AUNE), and later my role as a Core Faculty Member in AUNE's Education Department (home of the Critical Skills Program). All of these elements combined to provide the raw materials for what you hold in your hands.

It was my time in the woods that introduced me to facilitation. I learned that "teaching" is more about creating the right situations and asking the right questions than about being the smartest person in the room. I discovered and refined the art and science that are designing and processing experience. My time in that Essential school helped me to transplant that understanding to my classroom and gave me an understanding of what reflective practice means for teachers. It allowed me to see that "experiential learning" was more than just ropes courses—that it meant I was learning from my own teaching experiences in the same way my students were learning from their experiences in my room. Antioch and the Critical Skills Program gave me a system for creating more intentional, increasingly powerful experiences for my students and for unleashing the power of combined content and process instruction. Ultimately, Next Generation instruction is the sum total of all of those experiences, combined to create a synergistic Something New. My best hope is that you will take it, refine it further, and make it your own.

Acknowledgments

A number of individuals had a hand in making this book a reality. In addition to the individuals named throughout, I'd like to acknowledge and thank John Thomas for asking me questions I didn't want to answer; Heather Kiley for introducing me to the AYF's Framework and for sharing her knowledge and perspective; Susan Dreyer Leon for pointing out that, while I had accumulated a great deal of snow, I had failed to create a snowball; Peter Eppig for setting me on this path and supporting me as I found my own way; and Peg Smeltz for doing simply everything under the sun. Thanks to Cathy Hernandez, Hudson Perigo, Lisa Shaw, and Lisa Whitney at Corwin for answering question after question with humor and patience. Finally, to all of the unnamed educators and students who served as teachers and guides along the way, I offer my deepest thanks.

PUBLISHER'S ACKNOWLEDGMENTS

Corwin gratefully acknowledges the contributions of the following reviewers:

Norma Barber
Language Arts Teacher
Ukiah School District 80R
Ukiah, OR

Sara Coleman
High School Chemistry Instructor
Norwalk High School
Norwalk, IA

Nancy Foote
Teacher/Administrator
Higley Unified School District–Centennial
Gilbert, AZ

Peter Fox
Educational Consultant
Fox Learning Consultancy
Gilboa, NY

Janice L. Hall
Retired Associate Professor of Education
Utah State University
Logan, UT

Marty Krovetz
Professor Emeritus, San Jose State University
Director, LEAD/Coalition of Essential Schools
Santa Cruz, CA

Amanda McKee
High School Mathematics Instructor
Florence County #5 School District
Johnsonville, SC

Melissa Miller
Science Educator
Lynch Middle School
Farmington, AR

Betty Rivinus
Principal
Baker Prairie Middle School, Canby School District
Canby, OR

About the Author

 **Laura R. Thomas** is the current director of the Antioch Center for School Renewal (www.antio chne.edu/acsr/), the service division of the Department of Education, Antioch University–New England. Her web page can be viewed at www.antiochne.edu/ed/ed_faculty.cfm.

She has been working in and with innovative schools since 1993, first as a speech and theater educator and later as a coach and consultant. Laura's expertise lies in the support of system-wide change, the building of learning communities for both adults and students, and facilitative instruction. She is affiliated with the Coalition of Essential Schools and the School Reform Initiative (www.essentialschools.org) and recently served as copresident of the New Hampshire affiliate of Learning Forward (formerly the National Staff Development Council).

In addition to acting as a school change coach and leading workshops and institutes on a variety of topics, including the Critical Skills Program, assessment, and school change, Laura teaches graduate-level courses in assessment, facilitation, and social issues in education. She is currently engaged in developing degree concentrations in Next Generation learning and problem-based learning. Both series launched in the spring of 2012.

Introduction

WHAT THIS BOOK IS AND IS NOT

Forty students. There were 40 students in my fourth-block class. The block schedule—which I loved (and still appreciate) with a deep and powerful adoration—required that my entire Contest Speech class come to me during one block—fourth block—and I had no idea how I was going to teach a speech and debate class of 40 kids with completely different levels of experience and commitment. As I looked out on that classroom of energetic, smart, creative kids, I knew only one thing: I couldn't allow myself to mess it up.

Now, nearly 20 years later, I find myself thinking the same thing nearly every day, not because I'm facing 40 students but because I'm facing two—my own kids—and I'm realizing that the language of schools in the new millennium is the language that will shape the way they experience learning. At the same time, I'm facing rooms filled with educators who are looking for real, meaningful answers. And I'm talking with administrators who need to squeeze everything possible out of every single moment and every single dime of their professional development budgets—and who recognize that they (and their teachers and their students) haven't a moment to waste in useless edubabble or impractical advice. The faces may be different, but the stakes are no higher now than they were then. It's about kids—it's always been about kids—and they get only one trip through school. It's up to us not to allow ourselves to mess it up.

21st Century Skills. Innovation. Common Core. RTI. Differentiated Instruction. Technology Integration. Service Learning. Problem Solving. Place-Based Instruction. Critical Thinking. Inquiry. Collaboration. The new millennium has already been filled with the jargon of change. On the education front, this change has been marked by a paradoxical emphasis on improving student achievement (as measured by standardized assessments) while also increasing the level of rigor, community engagement, and real-world connections between content and process. Teach students to think—but be sure they score well on the standardized exams. Engage them in meaningful work—but be sure to cover every topic in the curriculum guide. Frustration grows when we try to serve both masters, but the wise educator will realize that it isn't an either/or proposition. Students engaged in rigorous, meaningful work *will* score well on exams. Students who are used to seeing complicated, unexpected problems (and who have successfully solved them in the past) don't panic when faced with unfamiliar ideas on standardized tests.

Experienced educators recognize that (at least the meaningful half of) this "new" way of educating, with its roots in the work of Mann and Dewey, has been shaped over time by educators at all levels seeking better, more engaging, more authentic ways of teaching. The purpose of this book is not to convince the reader that this perspective on education is valid. I assume you already hold this philosophical position to some degree and are ready to move beyond the theoretical and into the practical. These progressive (some would say constructivist) methods have different names today—problem- (or project-) based learning, service learning, inquiry-driven instruction, experiential learning, place-based education—but they all have at their center the same presuppositions:

1. Students learn best when they are working on meaningful tasks that connect content with context and experience.

2. Classrooms must be safe but challenging places where interdependence, risk taking, and reflection are not only encouraged but expected.

3. Teachers know how to shift the center of gravity in their classrooms from themselves to the students (Dewey, 1938). In short, teachers know how to facilitate.

It is the third assumption with which I am most concerned in this book, but I would be foolish to imagine that any one of these three can be fully separated from the others. Classrooms are systems in which each element depends upon the others much like natural systems. Changing one part of such a system requires attention to all parts of the system (Fullan, 2007). Systems thinking—the awareness that organizations are self-organizing entities that adjust themselves to maintain their own existence—applies to classrooms in the same way it applies to businesses, national parks, and schools of fish. Remove the wolves from Yellowstone, and the elk overpopulate and die of starvation, establishing a smaller population of elk that can survive in the new system. Schools of fish are governed by two simple rules: Stay in the middle of the group and don't get eaten. Each fish adjusts its position relative to the others in order to maintain its own position in the center and, therefore, survive. Students in our classrooms adjust their behavior based on who is in the room, what actions were last taken by the other students and the teacher, what the physical space requires of them, and what they most need in order to be "successful" (as they define success). We must look at all the elements of our classrooms in connection to each other in much the same way that naturalists must be attentive to an entire ecosystem rather than just one part (Wheatley & Kellner-Rogers, 1996).

fa·cil·i·ta·tor n

1. somebody who enables a process to happen, especially somebody who encourages people to find their own solutions to problems or tasks

2. an organizer and [a] provider of services for a meeting, seminar, or other event ("Facilitator," 2009)

Facilitation is a term not often applied to classroom instruction, particularly in traditional public schools. We talk about pedagogy, instructional strategies, classroom management, and assessment, but the term *facilitation* is most often heard in outdoor education settings. Looking at the first definition, however, can anyone deny that good teachers engaged in powerful work with their students are doing just that—enabling young people to complete meaningful tasks in service of a real problem and encouraging them as they do so? Next Generation instruction is the application of facilitation methods to the regular classroom.

This book is an action guide—a tool designed to be pulled off the shelf and used throughout the school year. Written with classroom teachers in mind, it draws on resources developed and used by practicing teachers and skilled facilitators from diverse professional settings. In short, I've culled tried-and-true strategies from across the continuum and combined them here for your use.

Meet the Facilitators

W hile I'll be drawing from my own experiences teaching theater, speech, and English in public and private schools, I've selected a number of experienced facilitators from whose classrooms I'll be drawing most of my examples. Since we'll be hearing from them quite frequently, it seems only logical that we share a bit of background about their experience. Many gained their primary training through Antioch University–New England's Critical Skills Program or through the Coalition of Essential Schools, though each has developed facilitation skills through a variety of experiences over time. Some have been teaching for decades; others are new to the profession. They teach in public and independent schools located in rural, urban, and suburban areas. While they teach different content and work with different students, they share a belief in the power of student-centered instruction as a path to full engagement in rigorous learning. Some will also frequently use the term *challenge* to describe a problem-based lesson that students solve individually, in small groups, or as a full learning community (McGrath, 2007). As you'll read, you'll find that each has a slightly different perspective on what it means to be a facilitative (Next Generation) instructor.

> 66 Some will frequently use the term *challenge* to describe a problem-based lesson that students solve individually, in small groups, or as a full learning community.
> —McGrath, 2007 99

Al Magnusson has been teaching science at Hampton Academy, a public middle school in Hampton, New Hampshire, since 1984.

What made you decide to change your instruction? It was not so much changing my instruction. I had come to teaching via coaching soccer first. I had coached for four to five years (at the varsity level) and then decided to take the "teaching/educating" from the soccer field to the classroom. I never had any formal teaching instruction until after I started teaching because I was certified under the [Critical Shortage Area] Alternative 4 Certification program. So my teaching had really developed from intuitive methods I had worked on with the soccer coaching.

What results have you seen? Motivated students. I'm always trying to find (student centered) activities that engage 100% of the kids, 100% of the "work" time. Students enjoy the praise they get from me (as we explore what successful self direction, collaboration and academic growth is all about) and that continues their motivation to equal or even do better. I utilize the old adage "Good, better, best . . . never let it rest, 'til the good is better and better is best." . . . Kids feed off this success, and the lessons—challenges—get stronger and more rewarding. Plus, this method helps me develop a distinct relationship with my students. Those relationships inevitably amplify the power of our community. When we have that, then the learning just takes off.

How has your teaching changed? Being able to read the student's needs, whether academic or skill based, and modify what we/they need to "work" on. Learning is all about having the students see the curriculum (again, academic or skill oriented) from different viewpoints, angles, etc., and then revisiting or spiraling the content so they get it. "Once and done" hardly ever, ever works, especially with abstract concepts. Being able to read this practically instantaneously and respond is the key to meeting the kid's needs. The real trick is doing this in the heterogeneous classroom; there needs to be something for the kids who've got it to do while others spiral . . . differentiation!

How do you feel when you use facilitative methods? How do I "feel"?????? Interesting question. I guess, I'd say . . . empowered and proud. I am the guide on the side rather than the sage on the stage. I consistently appreciate the feedback I receive from my students regarding the type of work they do in my classroom. They thoroughly enjoy my class because they are engaged and learning and understand what they are learning and why they are learning it. I feel empowered because I am empowering my students through student-centered work. This work also has to have a strong sense of real-world application for them to really want to learn it or understand the reason to learn it.

What advice would you give to someone just beginning this work? Start off at a pace where you are comfortable. Some people jump right in. I like to use the "rowing" analogy. You have to test the waters—row out a little, test one method, row back in. . . . But stay the course, be careful not to stop, keep rowing out and exploring, find things that work for you, that match your personality, your teaching style, and the age of the kids. Many teachers stop using these methods because they can't find the things that work for them fast enough, but take your time, document your progress, keep a simple reflective journal. There are some things that I have found just don't work well for me with my style and the kids' level.

Some teachers say, "Oh well, I do that stuff all the time." I often challenge that. Please find ways to embed "soft skill" progress (things like communication, collaboration, organization, self-management, etc.) with academic progress. This is where most people fall short. Yes, it takes a little longer to do these sort of things at first, but the payoff later is huge.

> 66 Some teachers say, 'Oh well, I do that stuff all the time.' I often challenge that. 99

AND, you can't do it all. Find those things that fit just right for you. Of course, there are those of you that will row out into the waters and put a motor on and try a bunch of things. This needs caution also—it can put too much on the kids and not provide them with a balance of academics and skill progress. They may not feel the proper flow and be overwhelmed.

Erin Hunter has been teaching carpentry to junior- and senior-level students at the River Valley Technical Center in Springfield, Vermont, since 2002.

What made you decide to change your instruction? Not so much change as refine. It was about the intentionality piece. Everyone said I was a good teacher, but I didn't know why—I was flying by the seat of my pants. It was random. I wanted to know what I was doing—to be intentional about what I taught and how I taught.

What results have you seen? I think that for me, when I first got into teaching, I knew what the state requirements were for my program: "By the end of the second year, cover this through this." The transition was to depth not breadth—getting students to walk away with knowledge they'll keep rather than an exposure to a lot and then they don't remember diddly-squat. That was the big transition in terms of shifting to this other way of teaching. It was more holistic. I always believed in teaching the person, not the content, but it gave me a framework for teaching depth, not exposure.

How has your teaching changed? The more I learn, the more I know that I want to be even more intentional. I am very clear about where I'm trying to go and how to get my students there. I love the bus analogy. I don't use "TripTiks"[1] anymore: "By June of year 2 I have to be here, so we're going to go this far today come hell or high water." Now I let the kids drive the bus, and if they want to stop and look at the giant ball of string, we do—but we still get where we need to get to by the time we need to.

How do you feel when you use facilitative methods? It's so freeing and empowering. I view it as a relationship—it's a learning relationship. Developing that relationship is very freeing because, if you're willing to give students a voice and power, they will make it very clear where they need to go and what they need to work on—and what I need to work on.

What advice would you give to someone just beginning this work? Don't be afraid. No fear. Don't be afraid to step outside your comfort zone if you're going to ask your students to do so. One of the things I see all the time is that when you're just not afraid of your students, if you respect them and you give them the same trust you want them to have in you, you can go places you never thought you could go. It sounds stupid, but trust the process. They'll help you to take it to levels you never thought you could. If you try to do it without them—if you try to control them and the process and everything—you'll exhaust yourself. If you're not afraid to be vulnerable and exposed, the results are worth it.

Caitlin Steele has 11 years of teaching experience, the last 5 teaching English to ninth-grade students at the Otter Valley Union High School in Brandon, Vermont.

How did you become a facilitative instructor? Through slow evolution over my full teaching career . . . a little intuition; some reading, observing, and asking questions; a few great trainings; and a lot of trial and error.

What made you decide to change your instruction to this way of teaching? I've never been much of a lecturer (though that style of instruction has its time and place). I think a good textbook can be an excellent instructional tool, but I've never limited a class to or by its text. I do believe that drill and practice are essential to developing some hard skills. I've always used a range of methods in my classes, but I've incorporated more and more facilitative instruction over the years, because I've found it to be the most effective way to engage all of my students in active learning. They can daydream while I yammer on, skim or just pretend to read any text I assign, and wait for the right answer to come to them rather than actively solve a grammar drill, but when I assign a creative, inquiry-based project that requires an individualized, concrete product in response, there is no lazy way out. Students have to work. Often in this context, they want to work, and I get to walk around offering support.

> 66 When I assign a creative, inquiry-based project that requires an individualized, concrete product in response, there is no lazy way out. 99

What results have you seen? As I've incorporated more and more facilitative instruction in my classes, I've seen more active learning. Students have asked better questions and more of them. I've had more students in my classroom voluntarily before school, after school, and during breaks in the school day; putting more time into their school projects; and pushing themselves to do their best and to make their best better. I've seen a higher level of achievement among a greater percentage of my students.

How has your teaching changed? Facilitative instruction requires much more planning up front. Students can thrive when given a great deal of freedom to demonstrate their learning in creative, individualized ways, but they need clear boundaries and expectations. I spend a lot of time planning lessons, tasks, and projects and then offering a variety of individualized verbal and written feedback to my students. And I make a point of reflecting on my methods afterwards. I rarely use exactly the same project in the same way twice, but am constantly tweaking and revising.

How do you feel when you use facilitative methods? The planning is a lot of work, but while teaching, I feel liberated. Once the class culture has been established and the project expectations have been made clear, the students do a lot of the teaching for themselves. I am free to circulate, check in, offer suggestions, ask questions, and guide rather than direct the class.

What advice would you give to someone just beginning this work? Find a team of colleagues and collaborate in this work. Brainstorm together. Bounce ideas off one another. Plan lessons and units. If you can, teach together. And absolutely take the time to reflect together. Be prepared for some ideas to flop, and have a sense of humor about it. Changing the way you teach is a challenging process. Co-conspirators can help you stay focused and inspired.

Bruce Perlow has been teaching 9th- to 12th-grade social studies at Otter Valley Union High School in Brandon, Vermont, since 2004.

How did you become a facilitative instructor? As I worked with a team to develop the Freshman Academy program at Otter Valley for the 2010–2011 academic year, we worked with Antioch University–New England's Center for School Renewal. During this time, we were introduced to and explored facilitative teaching ideas. These matched our beliefs about teaching and what we were hoping to accomplish with the Freshman Academy. I also took the Critical Skills course during the summer of 2010.

What made you decide to change your instruction to this way of teaching? My strong belief that this method of instruction results in true learning experiences.

What results have you seen? The most significant result I have seen is how much, once they embrace it, students enjoy the control and investment in their learning this gives them.

How has your teaching changed? I believe now more strongly than I ever have that intensive, collaborative team teaching is the most successful method for student learning.

How do you feel when you use facilitative methods? I feel good, albeit sometimes frazzled and overwhelmed, but mostly I feel that I am creating an opportunity for students to truly learn and be successful.

What advice would you give to someone just beginning this work? This is difficult work; don't underestimate it. Implement changes slowly; try one assignment, then one unit. To do this successfully takes a great deal of up-front planning and work.

Chris Lemieux has been teaching ninth-grade science at Otter Valley Union High School in Brandon, Vermont, since 2009.

How did you become a facilitative instructor? I attended Antioch University–New England from 2006 to 2008, where I was trained to use constructivist strategies and authentic lessons with my students.

What made you decide to change your instruction to this way of teaching? At Antioch, it became clear that facilitating rather than preaching from the chalkboard was a more effective way to engage high school students. I attended very traditional schools growing up, and I was looking for a better practice than what I had experienced as a student.

What results have you seen? Results have largely been positive, with some mixed results. Many students respond well to the freedom of assignment choice (and within certain parameters, content choice) and take more ownership of their work. There are some instances in which students have not responded well to more flexibility, and rather than rising to the challenge, they decided that lowering their personal bar was acceptable just to get minimum credit for coursework. In my experience, I would say that both the high-flying kids and the lower-achieving ones benefit from the individualization offered, as well as the extra attention that each kid can get from a teacher using these methods. My concern is primarily for those "middle-of-the-road" kids who don't have strong parental involvement and are happy to coast or

> 66 I think about my colleagues who teach in very traditional ways and how hard it is for them to break out of that; I then consider a 15-year-old who has experienced traditional schooling for 10 years and realize that it is very difficult for some of these students to know what to do with the different style of program. 99

slip through the cracks. While I am a huge proponent of facilitative instruction, some students require a more rigid structure to produce better work. I think about my colleagues who teach in very traditional ways and how hard it is for them to break out of that; I then consider a 15-year-old who has experienced traditional schooling for 10 years and realize that it is very difficult for some of these students to know what to do with the different style of program.

How has your teaching changed? I find myself being far more flexible in how and what I teach. When the students have serious questions, they are always covered in some way. It doesn't matter how far off-topic if gets as long as it is pertinent to science, the community, or the life of a student. I once shifted a week's worth of curriculum because I discovered that shockingly few of my students knew about the Japan earthquake/tsunami/nuclear disaster (which was still in full disaster mode at the time), and we did a mini unit on it. The kids were totally interested, and I bumped into a couple of parents that week who thanked me profusely for bringing this current event into my classroom.

How do you feel when you use facilitative methods? Personally, I find it energizing to be in this type of classroom. There is a significant amount of repetition in traditional teaching. In facilitating students to be self-motivated, the variety of topics covered is immense, and the questions get deeper and deeper. During a project-building session, I could talk to one student about electric cars, talk to another about debris in space, talk to another about how to change audio levels in a video project, and have several conversations about literally any topic covered in high school (and many not covered). As you can imagine, it's a good way to ensure a solid night's sleep for both the students and for the teacher.

What advice would you give to someone just beginning this work? Facilitative instruction is no more difficult than managing a traditional classroom, and it is far more fun. If you are willing to put in time and effort to get trained in the basics, it is a great investment for a teacher to make. My advice is that communication with parents is critically important. Parents raised in a traditional classroom will not know the value or the philosophies that underlie your work. The more you interface with parents, the more they will help to get the kids to buy in. It is also important to lean on your colleagues, especially those with more progressive teaching experience. Being able to successfully execute this type of classroom necessitates having a base of a strong classroom/school community. When students see the sense of community as role-modeled by their teacher and they understand that both teacher and parent will hold them accountable for their decisions, they will shine. And as the teacher, you will be amazed at the relationships that can develop between you and your students.

Louise Van Order Hodson has been teaching middle and high school math and science at the Compass School in Westminster, Vermont, since 2000.

How did you become a facilitative instructor? I enjoy learning more that way. . . . I had worked at camps and outdoor programs plus hands-on museums. I knew kids learn more when they experience things and find them on their own.

What made you decide to change your instruction to this way of teaching? I was never a very traditional teacher.

What results have you seen? The biggest change is kids think school is fun. That is a lot for a middle school kid.

How do you feel when you use facilitative methods? To be honest, sometimes bored. When the kids get fully engaged and are working on their own, I don't always know what to do.

What advice would you give to someone just beginning this work? Take time to really plan. When you put the work in up front, you don't have as much to do when it is happening. Clear expectations and guidelines make your job so much easier.

Jenn Huard is the inclusion facilitator and a learning specialist (special educator) at Souhegan High School in Amherst, New Hampshire, since 2007.

How would you describe your role at Souhegan? I serve as the case manager for students who have IEPs on our team, as well as coteach and codesign curriculum for all students on our heterogeneous team for English, science, social studies, and math. I also teach an academic support class that provides a chance for students to work on schoolwork, develop study and organizational skills, and receive reteaching and remediation. Academic support is available for all students to take, whether they have an IEP or not. Additionally, I have worked with our reading specialist, Beth Dunham, and taught intervention-level reading over the summer. I help teachers design curriculum that can challenge every learner.

How did you become a facilitative instructor? Prior to teaching, I worked in human services providing support to individuals who had traumatic brain injury and their families. I still provide home health services for one individual. I have worked with this amazing person since 1997. Human services, social work, and the medical field are very much like teaching. Every individual is different, and they all have different needs. What works for one will not necessarily work for another. We cannot expect the same achievement or growth from every individual. Whether we are discussing how one will recover from an operation or respond to the best-designed classroom lesson, everyone has unique needs, experiences, and accomplishments. My personal experiences as a student, parent, and human service professional helped me appreciate the importance of facilitation and other Coalition of Essential Schools principles. You need to know where you are and where you are going before you can figure out how you are going to get there.

What made you decide to change your instruction to this way of teaching? Since I came from a human services background, what is commonly referred to as *personalization* and *person-centered planning* is ingrained into my soul. After I decided to become a teacher, I began observing teachers across all grade levels and content areas. Careful observation not only of the teacher, but mostly of the students and how they responded, helped me truly understand the importance of facilitation, differentiation, behavior management, and, most importantly, engagement. If the students are not engaged and invested, there is not much hope of meaningful learning.

What results have you seen? When students are engaged, they *can* learn. When the information is relevant to the students, they *do* learn. Making all curriculum accessible to all students is vital. It would be criminal if you had a student who wanted to learn and was invested in the topic, but was unable to access the curriculum due to the lack of differentiation. Teachers need to be ready for any student that sits in their classroom. It's about being ready and prepared. When the teacher acts as the textbook and imparter of all knowledge, most students will be passively engaged at best. When the teacher acts as the facilitator for students to access knowledge and solve problems to create an understanding, the students are likely to not only be engaged but to retain what they learned because they experienced it.

How has your teaching changed? My teaching has changed by trying to place a deliberate focus on developing skills. The content knowledge can be the mode, but the actual target area should be a skill. Many facts are taught repeatedly through school. Many students do not remember what they learned the year prior, so we reteach it. This is done repeatedly, and yet we continually see that many students do not retain the facts. This is why I feel it is important for teachers to focus on developing transferable skills, such as problem solving, organizing, communication, or planning, and use the content as a mode to investigate those skills areas. Focusing on too much content has left our children with a lack of basic skills, and an overload of information means they are unable to remember most of what is taught.

A deliberate effort also needs to be made to use language and explain to students that grades are not something they get from a teacher—they are a representation of what they have learned in regard to the mastery of skills/ content accessed in a class. Additionally, it is important to have students monitor their own progress. Students need to take ownership of their learning, and they should always know where they stand in relation to their progress toward a goal.

> 66 Focusing on too much content has left out children with a lack of basic skills. 99

How do you feel when you use facilitative methods? When I use facilitation methods and the teachers I work with use them, I feel accomplished. I feel the most proud when the facilitative methods were so effective that students don't need to study to take a quiz, or look at their notes to give an answer about process or application, because they genuinely *know* the answers. They have experienced it to a point where they truly understand the concepts.

What advice would you give to someone just beginning this work?

1. Focus on transferable skills and use the less-is-more approach, breadth over depth. At Souhegan High School, we use Academic Learner Expectations (ALEs) to measure student growth. Our ALEs are Self- Directed Learner, Complex Thinker, Skilled Information Processor, Effective Communicator, Knowledgeable Person, Collaborative Worker, and Responsible Citizen. What employers need from workers is people who are creative; have ingenuity; are able to plan; and can communicate, follow through, organize, problem solve, and work collaboratively. It is easy to slip into focusing on content as we feel pressure for students to perform on high-stakes tests, but in my opinion, this is not best practice.

2. Observe other teachers often and ask others to observe you. Welcome constructive criticism.

3. Hold students accountable. Missing work is not an option. Not being engaged is not an option. Let the students know that you care too much to let them off the hook because you know they are capable.

Allison Robinson has been teaching middle school social studies at Monadnock Regional Middle/High School in Swanzey, New Hampshire, since 1996.

How did you become a facilitative instructor? I began thinking about changing the way I instruct when I began my master's program at

Antioch five years ago. Much of Antioch's instruction was critical skills based, and I enjoyed learning in that environment. The school also provided classes around learning how components of critical skills worked. After that, I was hooked.

What made you decide to change your instruction to this way of teaching? I always say that teachers tend to teach the way that they learn best. I like to be engaged in class, try things out, manipulate ideas, and bounce things off my classmates, but that was not the way I was taught to teach. Most social studies classes that I had were lecture based. Have the information doled out, write it all down, memorize it, and spill it back out again on a test. But at Antioch, they reminded me of the classes that I had enjoyed the most when I was a student . . . the class where we had to demonstrate the different types of government "isms" using a box of donuts or the class where we made a skit out of current events. Classes where I was integrally involved in the learning, where I did research and applied what I knew and then created a product that then showed my learning, were the ones I enjoyed the most. These were concepts surrounding Critical Skills, and they started to make so much sense. Then I thought about my own teaching: When were the students most engaged? Not when I was lecturing—that was for sure—and I did a lot of that my first years. As time when on, I found that projects and demonstrations that involved visualizing big concepts were more engaging to my students, and I began to incorporate them into my classes more. Allowing students to work together, solve problems, and *think* on their own make the concepts I wanted them to get stick better. Critical Skills gave me the vocabulary and the structure to make the things that worked best in my classroom work better.

> ❝ Classes where I was integrally involved in the learning, where I did research and applied what I knew and then created a product that then showed my learning, were the ones I enjoyed the most. ❞

What results have you seen? First of all, most of my students *like* social studies class, they like coming into class, they like what we do, and they like the "climate" of my classroom. I really like that. In the beginning, there is not much to look at that I can point out as results, but as the year goes on, my students ask better questions; they tend to make better connections between what we are learning about in class and what is going on in the world. They are better at explaining what/how they are thinking and better at asking for specific feedback that will help them. They tend to ask each other questions before they ask me. They are more independent and willing to think about things before looking for a quick solution.

How has your teaching changed? When I think of how I used to teach, it was more about the focus on acquiring content information. How many countries and capitals could I get them to memorize? I now look at my teaching as ways for them to practice the skills they need to learn and my content as the vehicle for them to acquire those skills. I look at my role less as the imparter of knowledge than as the person who guides them through the process of learning. I feel that I really get to know my students as individuals and how they learn, not just what they can show me on a test. I am more patient when they do not understand something and more willing to go back and look at a concept they didn't quite grasp the way I wanted them to because it is all a part of the learning process, even if we all have to do it again.

How do you feel when you use facilitative methods? Most of the time, I would say it feels good to be watching my students working so independently. Sometimes I feel bored. . . . I have nothing to do—well, nothing that is usually considered "teaching." Truthfully, I am constantly observing: How are students interacting with each other? Who is losing focus? Who seems to be struggling? Who is going beyond what I anticipated? This is where I feel like I really get to give students some individual attention.

What advice would you give to someone just beginning this work? Take the pieces that work for you and start to use them where they make sense for you. Theoretically, you could convert your entire classroom overnight into a collaborative community of learning, but that is not realistic for many of us. But the more pieces you begin to incorporate, the better it gets. It is a change in mind-set for you and your students because for many of them, your classroom may be the only place where these types of experiences are happening, and for you, it is a lot of thinking about why you are doing what you are doing or not doing, which is sometimes harder than just teaching it out straight.

Dan Callahan has been the technology integration specialist at Pine Glen Elementary School in Burlington, Massachusetts, since 2009.

How did you become an integration specialist? I'd been dabbling with different levels of technology integration for years in my own special education classroom. When looking for a job in Massachusetts, I connected first with administrators in my new district through Twitter. After I met my current principal, he decided to interview me for the integration position based on my knowledge and interests.

What made you decide to teach the way you do? I do my best to teach in a way that demonstrates respect and trust for my students. I first really started on that journey when I read Alfie Kohn's *Punished by Rewards.* Further reading and having the chance to talk with other educators from around the country and world has only reinforced that perspective, as well as helping me understand how technology use can support those efforts.

What results have you seen (in the practice of the teachers you work with)? I know that I'm getting somewhere with teachers when I see them start coming to me with ideas of their own based on tools I've introduced them to or ideas we've discussed. They may not always know how to get there, but they understand where they want to go and recognize that I can help them with that.

How has your teaching changed? My teaching has changed so much over the past decade. I was really a terrible teacher when I started, and it took me some time to adjust to the nature of running a classroom. Once I understood that, I was able to move on to using better strategies for working with students and figuring out how I could use technology to help with that.

> **❝** I'm in a constant state of amazement when I introduce students to new tools and just stand back and let them create what they want, how they want. **❞**

How do you feel when you use facilitative (student-centered) methods? I'm in a constant state of amazement when I introduce students to new tools and just stand back and let them create what they want, how they want. I've frequently found that the more opportunities they have to express their own creativity, the more powerful the final product turns out.

What advice would you give to someone just beginning this work? Using technology in your teaching will make your life easier in some ways, more difficult in others. It can allow for very easy collection of information, but that's pretty low on the scale of actual potential for devices when you get them into student hands. The real reward comes from giving students tools that allow them to find new ways to express themselves and then helping to guide them in a way that brings their vision to fruition.

NOTE

1. A "TripTik" is a road map provided by the American Automobile Association that outlines how far a traveler should expect to go in a specific day as well as important landmarks.

1

What Is Next Generation Instruction?

I did what I knew. And when I knew better . . . I did better.

—Maya Angelou[1]

Think for a moment about the word *teaching.* The images that emerge are probably reflective of your own academic experiences. Most likely, you imagine straight rows of desks with the teacher in front, sharpened number 2 pencils, copied worksheets, and textbooks. Some of you may remember a few projects, experiments, and field trips that inspired new understanding, but few will remember school as fundamentally those things. What if instruction, assessment, and community building had blended seamlessly into one another? What if assessments *taught* you something new—about yourself and about the content—and every instructional choice your teacher made led to a new understanding of what you knew and could do? What if each led to a stronger learning community, providing a platform for even more rigorous learning?

Now think about your own classroom. What if you could

- enhance the quality of the learning experience?
- assist students in learning how to learn?
- create learning that was lasting and transferable?

I view Next Generation instruction as being synonymous with facilitation, coaching, or acting as the "guide on the side" (as opposed to the "sage on the stage"). Ted Sizer, in writing what would become the foundational text of the Coalition of Essential Schools, referred to a shift away from the paradigm of "the teacher as the primary deliverer of educational services" to one in which the student acted as the worker and the teacher was the coach (Sizer, 1984/2004, p. 226). Long-time educational reformer Deborah Meier agreed that

> improved learning is best achieved by improving teaching and learning relationships, by enlisting the energies of both teachers and learners. . . . Human learning, to be efficient, effective, and long-lasting, requires the engagement of learners on their own behalf, and rests on the relationships that develop between schools and their communities, between teachers and their students, and between the individual learner and what is to be learned. (Meier, "Alternative Assumptions," 2000)

Students are continually asked to memorize and regurgitate—to parrot facts in order to achieve on standardized assessments—but are rarely asked to think. Now, I've yet to meet a teacher who entered the profession out of a deep and powerful desire to help students memorize meaningless factoids. Universally, we aspire to more for our students—we want them to become participatory citizens who are curious about the world around them. If we don't help them to become just that, they're going to find themselves prepared for a world that no longer exists. The best way to teach them to question, to evaluate, to problem-solve, and to communicate is to put them in situations where these skills are nonnegotiable while also teaching them how to do these things well (Wagner, 2008). The entire 21st century skills movement is based upon the reality that schools must move toward a "new pedagogy" based in active problem solving and engagement with material. "The world is changing," wrote Ken Kay (2010), director of the Partnership for 21st Century Skills. "Manual labor and routine tasks have given way to interactive, nonroutine tasks—even in many traditionally blue-collar occupations" (p. xvi). In the conclusion to their 2008 *Phi Delta Kappan* review of assessment across multiple countries, Linda Darling-Hammond and Laura McCloskey (2008) described what students "need to know to succeed in today's knowledge-based economy: the abilities to find, analyze, and use information to

> " Now, I've yet to meet a teacher who entered the profession out of a deep and powerful desire to help students memorize meaningless factoids. "

solve real problems; to write and speak clearly and persuasively; to defend ideas; and to design and manage projects" (p. 271).

As states across the country begin to implement the Common Core State Standards, we are recognizing that the standards themselves call for a different way of teaching. Since the curriculum is designed to encourage not only recall of information but also the application of this information, educators must find ways for students to dig more deeply into the material being taught (CCSSO, 2011). The pedagogical approaches most able to lend themselves to this application (problem-, project-, place-, and inquiry-based instruction, for example) require teachers to take on this new role as guide and resource. Posnick-Goodwin (2010) wrote about the impact of new standards in terms of skills, and her words can just as easily describe a new approach to content:

> The new standards have much more of a focus on application and making sure kids use the skills and strategies they learn. The new standards are more practical with less emphasis on learning skills and more on actually using those skills, thinking and doing. There should be more discourse in the classroom, more opportunities for kids to talk to each other. (Posnick-Goodwin, 2010)

We are more likely to achieve this discourse and application when we give our students not only the chance to gain new content knowledge but also the confidence to engage with one another without depending on the teacher to act as the instructional linchpin. The emerging theme is clear—we need to rethink our methods if the next generation of students is going to be successful.

Over and over across time, philosophy, and context, we hear the same thing: "The learner does the learning" (Danielson, 2010). This is just as it should be. But teacher-preparation programs often create educators who teach the way teachers (in recent memory) have always taught—through lectures, worksheets, and textbooks. While some programs may offer theoretical training in constructivist methods (i.e., problem- or project-based learning, service learning, etc.), the methods modeled by professors are more likely to reflect traditional pedagogy. While these methods still have a place, they no longer represent the full spectrum of pedagogy. Peter Senge (2000) wrote:

> If a child's primary orientation in school becomes pleasing a teacher, this attitude will draw attention away from developing the capacities for more rigorous self-assessment. Meanwhile, a cornerstone of lifelong learning is the capacity for objective self-assessment—the ability to judge for yourself how well you are

doing. In effect, teacher and student collude in shifting the developmental burden from self-assessment to pleasing others. The result can be adults who spend their careers currying favor rather than doing something they truly regard as meaningful. Few educators would espouse this, but the system of specialization and control produces it. (p. 44)

Even well-intentioned educators, trained in the use of different methods, may be find themselves tied up in the textbooks, curriculum guides, standards, and other demands placed upon them.

BOX 1.1   A NOTE ABOUT TECHNOLOGY

For many, Next Generation instruction is synonymous with technology integration. While technology is certainly an important tool in the 21st century, it is not the only tool a Next Generation instructor has in the toolbox. While reference will be made throughout the text to situational usages of technology, the more important element is the number of times you *won't* see technology used by our instructors. According to technology integration specialist Dan Callahan, "Sometimes the lesson is great as it is and you shouldn't use technology. It's like anything else—look at your goals and your options and figure out what is a good fit." If you're not currently using any technology at all—if you don't even know how to use the tools available to you—then of course you need to take a hard look at what you might want to do differently and why you're not using what you have. Are you unaware of what's available? Do you lack training? Are you afraid of breaking something or looking foolish? Start by using your technology for your own professional learning—explore Twitter or YouTube to learn about something that you're interested in. Play with your interactive whiteboard. Ask colleagues you trust to show you what technology they're using—ask a student you trust the same question. Instead of starting out thinking "How can I use this for instruction?" start out asking yourself "How can this help me learn something I want to know?" Begin as a learner rather than as an instructor, and you'll have better results. Dan says,

> The challenge is trying to build resilience in teachers. There's a lot of talk about kids being "digital natives," but I'm not a fan of that term. I don't think kids know any more than we think they do. They know the stuff they know, and they know it very well, but there's a lot they don't know. They know what they know because they had a reason to learn it. They'll figure it out because it has a value for them. The biggest (technological) difference between adults and kids is that kids are willing to try again when things don't go right. When teachers try something—a website, say—and it doesn't work, and then they'll blame it on "Technology" writ

large. It's not technology; it's the site. Find a better site. It's really a matter of training teachers to do what the kids do. Lots of teachers use the tool "ask three before me." Wouldn't it make sense to do the same thing with the technology—especially if it would improve instruction?

In short, technology is a tool to do a job better. It's not the job itself.

There is a moment, sometimes, when a teacher recognizes that she's working a lot harder than her students. This blinding flash of the obvious can lead either to an abandonment of the profession or to a change in philosophy (or another last-minute Google search for lesson plans and activities!). The wise educators—the ones who choose to remain in the classroom— recognize that this way of teaching is exhausting, unsustainable, and not terribly effective for students. They then seek a way to shift the heavy lifting onto the shoulders of those who should rightly be carrying the load—the students. It is in the process of making this shift that they discover a new level of rigor, engagement, passion, and relevance. A new pedagogical world awaits those who are willing to make the change.

> **" There is a moment, sometimes, when a teacher recognizes that she's working a lot harder than her students. "**

WHAT ARE THE PURPOSES OF NEXT GENERATION INSTRUCTION?

The purposes of Next Generation instruction, to restate the definition from the introduction, are simply these:

- To intentionally structure quality learning experiences
- To assist students in finding new ways of taking responsibility for their learning
- To aid students in creating changes (in both habit and content knowledge) that are lasting and transferable

In order to understand Next Generation instruction, with its roots in facilitation and experiential learning, we need to understand the nature of experience. We all have experiences every day. We get up when the alarm goes off, or we hit the snooze button (and are either on time or late for work). We fill the gas tank or we don't (and either reach our destination or find ourselves stranded on the side of the road). Sometimes we think about the choices we make and their connected results, and then these events become learning experiences. Sometimes we don't take the time for that reflection, and then . . . we don't learn. The difference between the two (an experience versus a *learning* experience) was described by Kolb (1984) via the "elements of a learning experience." (A full exploration of the varied models for experiential learning would require another book completely—and that book has already been written by a number of other authors.) Kolb described an experiential cycle that includes the following:

- Concrete experience
- Observation of and reflection on that experience
- Application of abstract concepts to those reflections and observations
- Testing of new ideas based on that application

For example, I may realize that I never wake up on my own before 7:30 and that the drive to the airport will take 90 minutes. I will use that knowledge to make plans for catching a 9:00 AM flight. I will set my alarm to ensure sufficient time to wake up, dress, and catch the flight with sufficient time to park and make my way through the security gauntlet. This process—"getting to my flight on time"—is a *concrete experience* in itself. Once I'm safely seated on the plane, I may take time to *observe and reflect* on the success or failure of my plans. Was I scrambling to get to the gate on time? Was I overly rushed? Appropriately organized with all the documentation needed to fly in the 21st century? I will *apply abstract concepts* such as different routes to the airport, different airlines or airport choices, or a streamlined plan for getting dressed in the morning to see if there might be a better way to approach the process in the future. I will then adjust my future preflight plans to factor in new knowledge gained from this specific experience and *will test that new idea* the next time I travel.

Antioch's Critical Skills Program applies a similar model to classroom instruction, documenting a two-tiered experience in which students do the following:

1. **Engage** in a task (or "challenge").

2. **Exhibit** their learning.

3. **Reflect** on the process and knowledge used and gained.

4. **Transfer** that new knowledge and skill to different situations.

And in which teachers take the following actions:

1. **Design** learning experiences, focusing on both content and process skills.

2. **Coach** students as they engage in the experience and exhibit their learning.

3. Provide **feedback** (in concert with student reflection) about areas for future growth and skills attained.

No matter which model of experiential learning seems most aligned with your own background, the commonalities are clear. Student learning experiences can be carefully crafted to produce desired learning outcomes, but this learning will take place only if opportunities are provided for students to assess the content and quality of their learning and to plan to transfer that learning into future experiences.

Many classrooms currently provide problems for students to solve, projects to create, interesting questions in which to engage, and opportunities for exhibitions of one sort or another. The Common Core State Standards and related inquiry-driven instructional methods (e.g., International Baccalaureate. problem-, project-, or placed-based learning; service learning) will require more of this in the future. As we move toward these more student-centered methods, we must be mindful of and attentive to the reflection and transfer elements of experience. These key elements are the most important, because reflection and transfer are the moments in which learning occur—the moments in which students understand and integrate their learning into their real lives. Skilled facilitators are prepared not only to ask the right question at the right time but also to explicitly structure assignments and learning tasks to build in opportunities for reflection and transfer. They skillfully guide students through their experiences, calling to mind the old saw about being "the guide on the side" instead of "the sage on the stage."

> **"** These key elements are the most important, because reflection and transfer are the moments in which learning occur. **"**

The elements of this process have been combined into the framework for Next Generation instruction (see Figure 1.1), which will serve as the spine of this book. It has been adapted with permission from the work of outdoor and adventure educators at the American Youth Foundation.

The foundation of the framework is the collaborative learning community (CLC). The CLC is more than a cooperative environment, more than basic kindness and courtesy (though those are certainly important elements). It is an intentionally created classroom culture in which all the students (and adults) are able to make important contributions based on their unique skills and talents (McGrath, 2007). It's the result of careful planning throughout the life of the class, both as a separate task and as the result of your instruction and assessment. In the next

Figure 1.1   Framework for Next Generation Instruction: Overview

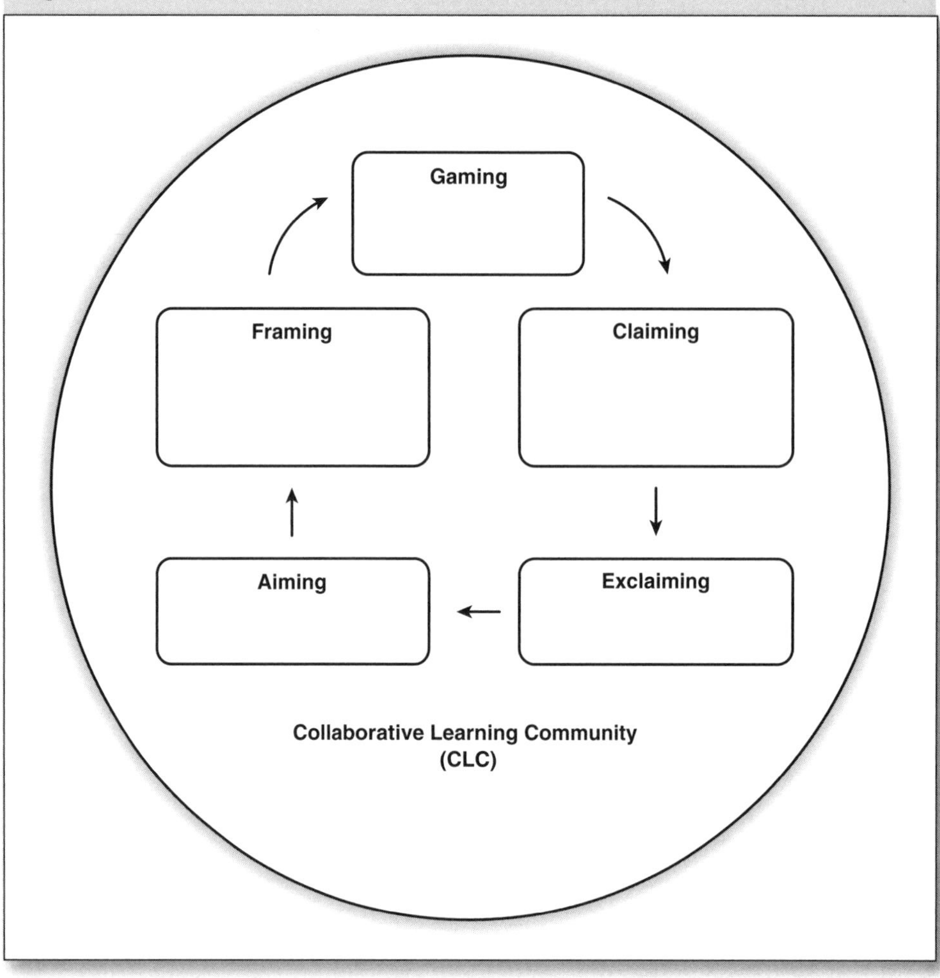

chapter, I'll describe the attributes of the CLC as well as the steps necessary to build it in more depth.

NOTE

1. *Jet*;1/30/95, Vol. 87 Issue 12, p. 51.

2

Laying the Groundwork

Building a Collaborative Learning Community

I learned, of course, that community is vital and important, but it is also terribly difficult work for which we are not well prepared; at least I was not. I learned that the degree to which a person yearns for community is directly related to the dimming of memory of his or her last experience of it.

—Parker Palmer, 1987, p. 20

Before planting a garden, the wise gardener prepares the soil carefully, with an eye toward the crops to be planted, the existing soil quality, what was grown there previously, and the success of last year's efforts. Similarly, before we can move into the specific elements of Next Generation instruction, we must step back and prepare the environment in which we will be working. The foundation of Next Generation instruction lies in a positive, supportive classroom community. Students must feel safe if they are going to take the risks required to be successful in a Next Generation classroom. Creating that sense of safety is your first task as a Next Generation instructor.

So what do we mean by *collaborative learning community* (CLC)? According to Antioch University–New England's Critical Skills

Figure 2.1   Framework for Next Generation Instruction: Collaborative
Learning Community

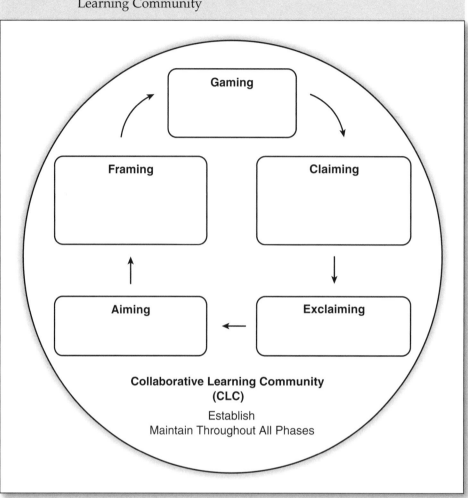

Program, a CLC is a "purposefully structured and actively maintained
classroom culture within which teachers and students take on full membership in support of the contributions of each individual member"
(McGrath, 2007, p. 19). Let's take that apart—there are a lot of words in
that definition.

First off, the CLC is *purposefully structured and actively maintained*—
it's planned in advance, with an eye toward sustainability, and it's a key
piece of the ongoing work of the students and teachers. When most
people think about building a learning community or team building,
they envision kids doing get-to-know-you games, tossing a ball across a
circle, or stepping through hula hoops or over ropes. As you'll read
later, there *is* a place for those kinds of activities in building your CLC,

but there's a lot more to maintaining the CLC than just coming up with a new game two or three times a week. Purposefully structuring your CLC means planning it in the same way that you plan your lessons—building upon assessments, structuring the work so that students can be successful but challenged, and always looking for new ways to get the point across—rather than just following the curriculum guide, looking to see what chapter comes next, or searching the Web to see what others have done.

> **"** Classroom culture, just like school culture, is simply 'the way we do things around here.' **"**

Secondly, CLC is a *classroom culture.* Classroom culture, just like school culture, is simply "the way we do things around here" (Deal & Kennedy, 1983). It is the rituals, traditions, expectations, and experiences you and your students share together every day. In the CLC, however, the culture is created intentionally, with an eye toward inclusivity, interdependence, and safe challenges. Furthermore, it is maintained by both the teachers and students. The CLC isn't something that happens behind the scenes; it isn't the responsibility of the teacher alone (at least, beyond the second or third day of school). It is something in which *teachers and students take on full membership,* an attribute of the community that is assessed and discussed frequently and openly.

Finally, the collaborative learning community functions *in support of the contributions of each individual member.* This idea is surprising to some. After all, if we're talking about collaboration, then shouldn't we be supporting the group over the individual? There's no *I* in *team,* right? This notion undervalues the depth of group and individual effort that must be expended before the tremendous power of the CLC can be harnessed. Groups are made up of individuals, and individuals need to feel important and valued if they are to continue to engage in the group. The fact of the matter is that an individual may agree to cooperate without fully owning his or her place and power within the group. "If the group doesn't value me, I may still show up at the table (particularly if the teacher requires it), but I won't do more than the bare minimum. Heck, I may not even do that. Why should I?" Interdependence occurs when we intentionally share a transparent commitment to the success of every individual in the group. It's not just about supporting one another. It's about requiring the consistent, ongoing engagement of every member of the class toward a larger goal.

Behavioral psychologist Abraham Maslow put forward his perspective on those reasons back in the early 1940s when he published his hierarchy of needs (Maslow, 1943). While the concept of Maslow's hierarchy may seem tangential to our purposes here, it certainly helps us begin to understand the roots of human behavior. Essentially, Maslow believed that human beings seek to satisfy their needs in a particular order, beginning with the most basic (food, safety, shelter), then moving on to security (freedom from threat of harm, assurance of stability), then in the social realm (friendship, connections with others, love), on to self-respect (autonomy, feelings of personal worth), and finally seeking the sense of achieving full potential that comes with self-actualization.

So what does that mean for you and your emerging skills as a classroom facilitator, working with possibly new curricula and new instructional methods? It's simple. If students in your class lack immediate basic needs (if they are hungry or thirsty or cold) or if they are feeling insecure about their safety, they simply won't be able to focus on the higher social and self-respect level efforts required by the CLC and the accompanying Common Core and the Next Generation instructional methods—and your budding facilitation efforts will fail.

I can imagine that, at this point, many readers are thinking, "Well, lots of my students are hungry during the day, and many of them are insecure about their lives—their parents may be unemployed or divorcing or there may be illness or death in the family. This doesn't sound like it would work for my students." Rest assured, by building and maintaining a strong CLC, you and your students can actually help to meet some of these needs despite outside forces. The important thing here is to recognize that students are trying to get their own needs met all the time and that they *will* seek to move up through the hierarchy as each level's needs are met. They may make poor choices as they strive to do so (theft as a means to eat or to ensure some level of social compliance for example), if they see no other way forward. However, the classroom can become a safe harbor for those students who wouldn't otherwise experience safety on a consistent basis. If you and their peers can make *positive* opportunities available and expected, those examples will become the "path of least resistance," providing safe and fulfilling ways to get needs met. Once students are full and safe, they'll seek to connect with one another because that's what people do when they're full and safe. That connection—the fulfilling of social level needs—is where the CLC begins.

RECOGNIZING THE COLLABORATIVE LEARNING COMMUNITY

So what does the collaborative learning community look like? In my high school classroom, it looked like students working together in mixed groups—different ages, different areas of expertise, different personalities—to achieve both individual and group goals. It was busy hands, concentration, laughter, and 90 minutes flying by with unimaginable speed. It was open conversation about what we were doing well and why—and what we needed to change if we were going to succeed. In Erin Hunter's carpentry classroom at River Valley Technical Center in Springfield, Vermont, it looks very much the same—busy hands, laughter, concentration, and focused work—but it also looks like proud smiles as students learn skills they never imagined mastering; lead without being bossy; and confront differences with respect, honesty, and good humor. According to Caitlin Steele, a member of the High School Freshman Academy team in Brandon, Vermont,

> The most telling thing I saw was that our students wanted to be in our classroom space. They would show up individually with questions or in groups to work on projects before school, during break. Some would leave lunch to come to class early, and others would stick around after school. Our students who were on the student council often chose to do their committee work in our room. These outside-of-class times were social and friendly, but it was telling that ours was a space kids chose when they wanted to get something done.

As you surely noticed from the examples given above, no matter the school culture, teaching style, geography, student age, subject area, or teacher, CLCs have elements in common. They are not, however, exactly the same—and they are all created in unique ways. Each CLC will include rituals and traditions that combine distinctive elements of each classroom with long-standing experiences anticipated by incoming classes of students. Class trips to a specific destination (e.g., the seventh grade always takes a trip to Washington, D.C., in the spring, sixth graders always hold a toy drive before winter break, seniors camp on the football field the night before their last day, classes compete in a hallway-decorating contest as part of homecoming, no one walks on the school crest inlaid in the floor of the school entry), grade-level projects (the Romanticism notebook in 11th-grade English, the egg-drop competition in 8th-grade science), and annual events (spring picnic, fall pumpkin carving, the school carnival) can build common expectations and experiences that provide benchmarks for students. They can point to these rites of passage as evidence that they are part of a community and that they hold a specific place within that community.

Additionally, each community of students will need to create their own rituals and ways of being together. These "in jokes," *when they include every individual in the community,* can bind the CLC together. It goes without saying that any ritual can become powerfully destructive if even a single student is left on the "out" side of the joke. Humor builds the community only when it isn't at the expense of the dignity or pride of one of its members.

Some of the indicators of a healthy collaborative learning community include the following:

- Students know to expect unique classroom rituals and traditions.
- Full-value contract/classroom expectations are posted and referred to frequently.

- Furniture is arranged to support discussion among students (in a circle or circles, grouped desks, or other flexible arrangements).
- Classes begin with check-ins, both formal and informal, focused on how students are doing personally as well as academically.
- The teacher is responsive to and interested in student feedback about the content and process of the coursework.
- Teachers and students laugh together.
- Students take risks and support one another in reaching goals.

STAGES OF BUILDING AND MAINTAINING A COLLABORATIVE LEARNING COMMUNITY

In a perfect world, I would now present you with a checklist entitled "How to Build Your Collaborative Learning Community." It would have six or seven steps, be prettily formatted, and offer a complete road map to creating and maintaining your CLC. Unfortunately, your CLC will be made up of people, people are notoriously unpredictable, and unpredictability doesn't lend itself well to road maps. It does, however, make things a lot more interesting. So, in support of the interesting journey that you are about to undertake, I can offer you a general sense of where you're going to go. Not so much a "take Route 101 72 miles, then head south on I-93 for 3.7 miles, and you'll reach your destination in 90 minutes," but more a set of landmarks that you'll pass along the way. For our purposes, we will use five stages as described by the Critical Skills Model of Instruction (McGrath, 2007).

> 66 By intentionally offering opportunities for students to find out information about each other as people rather than as 'types' (or previous reputations), we can interrupt the pattern and lay the foundation for students to become more than they have been in the past.   99

Stage 1: Knowledge/Communication. This earliest stage of community development is almost two separate stages. If we are to work together, then we must first discover specific facts about other group members. For children, it is the number of pets and siblings; for adults, it is job roles and outside interests. Overwhelmingly, however, it is about the willingness to ask, to share and to listen, to interact with other group members in both a professional and a (somewhat) personal way. In secondary classrooms, this stage (left to its own devices) involves finding out who is in the room and determining relative social standing in order to create a "pecking order." By intentionally offering opportunities for students to find out information about each other as people rather than as "types" (or previous reputations), we can interrupt the pattern and lay the foundation for students to become more than they have been in the past. Activities such as partner introductions, pinwheels, personality scavenger hunt, Compass Points/ North-South-East-West, and I Like People Who can be useful at this stage. (See the end of this chapter and Chapter 6: Tips, Activities, and Tools for Next Generation Instruction for more information on these and other useful activities.)

Stage 2: Cooperation. As group members become familiar with one another, they begin to engage politely around the work. They follow all the appropriate rules, do the tasks necessary, and share resources—in short, they play nice. Many group-development models view this stage as the pinnacle of growth. I believe it to be the earliest sign that positive growth is occurring and that the group *might* one day become fully effective. A group at this stage may complete work assigned, but it will not produce brilliance, innovation, or inspiration. It will be mildly functional at best, perfunctory at worst. The tasks you give your students to do at this stage should be low risk and low stakes—building vocabulary lists, creating posters or personal reference materials, reviewing previous material, practicing processes they will need later, or finding out where important materials are kept in the classroom.

Stage 3: Trust. Typically, as groups work cooperatively, someone pushes. This may take the form of teasing another group member, asking a tough or probing question, or clashing with another personality. Any such crisis can

> 66 Trust comes as a result of a risk taken successfully and that doesn't always happen on its own. 99

set the stage for individuals to build trust in the group. Real group identity emerges beyond the identity defined by the task or tasks assigned. Individuals discover that the group is a safe place, that risks are valued and expected, and that they can go out on a limb without expecting another group member to follow with a saw. Trust in the group and its individual members is the common ground on which powerful work can be grown. Unfortunately, trust comes as a result of a risk taken successfully, and that doesn't always happen on its own. You may find that you need to "ramp up" the level of risk intentionally in order to jar the students out of the cooperation stage. This may mean creating a messier problem for students to solve, offering a trickier task, or choosing to make materials scarcer or harder to find. It will also require your best facilitation skills, and those can be learned only through practice. (Don't worry—we'll cover that later.)

Stage 4: Collaboration. Here the group begins to experience synergy. The work takes on a life of its own and is done enthusiastically and energetically. Watching a collaborative group, one notices that there seem to be no preassigned roles or responsibilities; rather, individual tasks are carried out by the individual with the time, ability, or proximity to do so. It is many hands working—perhaps silently, perhaps with a great deal of chatter and excitement—to do more than is required. Truly collaborative groups create masterpieces of all varieties. They are invested in and proud of their process and of their products.

Stage 5: Maturation and Maintenance. As the classroom community continues to exist, its collaborative spirit grows exponentially. The classroom community is owned by its individual members and seeks out ways to be useful and to do important work. A spirit of empowerment and excitement prevails, even in the face of challenges.

CREATING THE COLLABORATIVE LEARNING COMMUNITY

While there are multiple models for group development, each illustrating a slightly different perspective, the CLC described above represents a fairly universal set of experiences that you'll certainly recognize from your own classroom. The following will explain steps you should take to move your students through the three stages that are foundational to Next Generation instruction in the classroom:

1. Knowledge/Communication

2. Cooperation

3. Trust

Note that this journey is not linear. Development of trust occurs from the first moment your students arrive in your classroom. Your students must know that you will protect them emotionally, that you have their best interests at heart. From there, they can begin to build trust in one another—but they can't trust you if they don't know you, and vice versa. Early cooperative activities provide a springboard from which students can learn about one another, build trust, and prepare to launch themselves into the next level of work—collaboration. They do so in an environment in which all students are known well, know what is expected of them, and can count on the others in the community to behave supportively and

> 66 Your students must know that you will protect them emotionally, that you have their best interests at heart. 99

respectfully. Collaboration and maturation are the fruits of your labor and are maintained by ongoing meaningful work, reflection, and high expectations—but we'll get to that in the next chapters.

In these earliest phases (when groups first form), we typically observe a honeymoon period in which students seek low-level information about one another. Names, basic social information, and interests are the fodder for conversation. Group members focus on the things they have in common and are on their best behavior. The goal is smooth, polite interaction with minimal risk. Excitement is high, but so is anxiety. There is a great deal of social complexity at this stage. Few are certain of where they fit into the group, and this anxiety may trigger a strong desire to *fight* (assert dominance), *flee* (withdraw from the group fully), *flock* (create cliques), or *freeze* (disengage completely) (Corrie, 2003).

Planning ahead so that students immediately find answers to their most pressing questions can decrease the level of social complexity, thereby decreasing the likelihood that any of those behaviors will be triggered. What questions are pressing? Some are very concrete:

- Where will I sit?
- Where do I put my coat and/or bag?
- What if I have to go the bathroom?
- What should I bring with me?

Others are more abstract and tap into our insecurities and fears:

- Will I know anyone?
- Will the teacher like me?
- Am I wearing the right thing?
- Is this going to be a safe place for me?
- Will this class be fun?
- Will the work be too hard?

Wise educators will invest time and energy in this work during the early days of the course in a variety of ways, including games, formal introductions, informal interactions, and explanation of course syllabi and expectations (more about this below). The classroom facilitator will choose to do this work in nontraditional ways, slowly acclimating students to a new way of being, one based on inquiry and problem solving. The specific ways in which this is done will vary according to the teacher, the students, and the course and will reflect the essence of the classroom culture to come. At Souhegan High School in Amherst, New Hampshire, says learning specialist Jenn Huard,

> We do a variety of getting to know each other and working cohesively activities. I have used School Reform Initiative protocols,

such as the Compass Points, to allow students to learn about each others' differences and gain an understanding of what they need and how they respond in collaborative work. Once students learn to accept and appreciate one another, and possibly even understand where they are coming from, they can begin to work together cooperatively. We use a variety of activities such as your standard Charades and Pictionary; the Movie Game; lots of sharing in whips, such as scary memories, after high school hopes, and embarrassing moments; and creating bucket lists. Also, giving students a challenge such as how to get across a given area using only two pieces of wood creates cooperation within a group.

In Erin Hunter's carpentry program at River Valley Technical Center in Springfield, Vermont,

> It all starts with classic get-to-know-you name games and team-building activities that are very low risk. Names, where you're from, that stuff, since these kids come from five schools that have to be integrated into one learning community. That's everything. We spend quite a bit of time on the questions "Why did you take carpentry? Why did you take this program?" so they can identify their commonalities and their common ground—we're here for a common reason and a common goal.

Erin starts the first days by greeting students at the door by name. She may prepare a "do now" activity like an interest survey or learning-style inventory, or she may let the group remain unstructured until everyone arrives. At that point, depending on the group, she may select any one of six activities in her "bag of tricks," based on student energy and comfort levels. "The goal," she says, "is laughter. A light activity with a high degree of success. Something nonthreatening in which everyone is on the same level and is equally nervous." Erin participates to show students that she is willing to laugh and get involved, to show that she'll accompany them in risk taking, and to let them know that she's accessible. She is building trust on multiple levels while also building knowledge and communication.

The team at Otter Valley in Vermont takes a direct approach, collectively saying that

> we spent much of the first two weeks of the school year actively building our community through team-building games and reflection. We reorganized our students a few times a day, teaching some lessons to the whole class, some to ever-changing groups. And though we sometimes allowed students to choose their partners

when doing group work, we often actively separated them from their friends. By the end of the year, some students acknowledged aloud that they'd made more friends through working closely with kids they'd known only peripherally for years.

Technology integration specialist Dan Callahan at Pine Glen Elementary School, Burlington, Massachusetts, has suggested that class wikis, webpages, and blogs can also be useful in providing both an early project, a medium for creating a sense of classroom identity, and a long-term tool for communication and collaboration.

This "cocktail party" phase of group development (stages 1 and 2—Knowledge/Communication and Cooperation) can last hours, days, or weeks depending on the expected life span of the group. It is a comfortable stage, and many group members will work hard to hold on to it. It is also, however, not a very productive stage. (There's a reason that cocktail parties go on for only a couple of hours!) Those classrooms that are largely "sit and get" experiences, with teacher-centered instruction and little necessity for students to do more than act as recipients of information, may never move beyond this stage of low student engagement. (Many college classrooms never even arrive at it!) In this stage, students will, at best, go through the motions of collaboration, but they will not, as a rule, strive to produce high-quality work unless driven by outside forces (e.g., parental pressure, college admissions expectations, high intrinsic motivation) because they simply don't trust one another—or you—enough to take the risks that high-quality engagement requires. Unfortunately, this level of group development is too often the status quo in high school classrooms. Moving beyond this stage requires us to agree to take risks together.

> 66 Each term, each period, each day, I had to remind myself to see who was really in the room with me—not who had been there before, but who was there at that moment—so I could adjust my expectations accordingly. 99

When asking students to take the risks that are both the result of and the mechanism by which trust is built, we must first understand the nature of risk itself. We all experience risk from our own points of view. We view some activities as frightening, others as less so, but our determinations are made based on our own histories. We know that all of our students are unique, with their own sets of experiences, and we must use our early days together to get to know them well so that we can keep them safe and challenged. In my own classroom, teaching speech to terrified 9th–12th graders in a totally heterogeneous setting, I had to be very careful not to assume that this period's response to the assignment was going to be the same as last period's. Block 1 was filled with sleepy students who didn't want to role-play (or even get out of their seats), but Block 2 was filled with energetic, silly 9th graders who loved to jump up and create absurd examples of the content. Block 3 in my first term included two students who had suffered significant personal trauma, which required me to rethink the level of risk appropriate for everyone in the room, but the same period in the second term had some complacent kids who needed me to push them toward a higher level of risk and some shy students who needed all the support I could offer. Each term, each period, each day, I had to remind myself to see who was really in the room with me—not who had been there before, but who was there at that moment—so I could adjust my expectations accordingly. Sounds impossible, I know, but if you've ever just *known* that what you had planned wasn't going to work, based only on the high or low energy you felt from the students when they entered your room, then you understand.

The School Reform Initiative refers to zones of comfort, risk, and danger as nested circles (see Figure 2.2). The innermost of these reflects our most safe activities. Think for a moment about the activities in which you feel most confident, safe, and secure. For me, one activity in my "Comfort" zone might be going to the beach. It's something I've done often, I enjoy it, and I have no insecurity about my ability to do it and enjoy doing it.

Figure 2.2 Zones of Relative Risk Taking

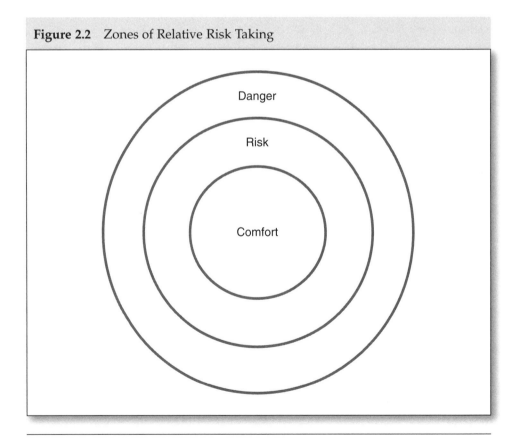

Source: National School Reform Faculty, n.d. Used with permission.

The second sphere marks those activities that challenge us but in which we are willing to engage anyway. It is our risk zone, the zone in which we may feel uncertain and a bit afraid. This is the zone in which we are able to

> 66 If you were unsure, but moved forward anyway, you were probably working in your risk zone. 99

learn most powerfully. To extend my earlier example, I would place taking my small children camping at the beach for a week, by myself, in this zone. I would feel uncomfortable, increasingly so as the date of the trip drew nearer. I might try to make excuses not to go, might pray for bad weather to cancel the trip. Ultimately, with trepidation, I'd go. I'm used to working in my risk zone and, even though I don't love it, I'm self-aware and mature enough to be able to manage. At the end of the week, I'm certain I would feel proud and happy that I'd done it. I might even be willing to do it again. Think about experiences that you've had that you would place here—performing, running a marathon, deciding to have a baby, getting married, purchasing a home, walking into your classroom as a new teacher for the first time . . . the specifics of the experience don't matter as much as the response it inspired in you. If you were unsure but moved forward anyway, you were probably working in your risk zone.

The final circle marks the zone of danger. Activities in this sphere trigger the amygdala, that portion of the brain that triggers a fear response and interferes with reasoning. When an individual is working in the danger zone, he will respond as though under threat—in much the same way he might respond should his lowest-level needs (remember Maslow?) remain unmet. As noted above, the powerful, instinctual desire to *fight* (assert dominance), *flee* (withdraw from the group fully), *flock* (create cliques), or *freeze* (disengage completely) may lead to unpredictable behavior, aggression, or withdrawal from the group.

So it seems clear: When you begin to move toward Next Generation instruction, start in the safe zone and move your students into the risk zone. Avoid the danger zone. Simple, right? The problem, as you've probably anticipated, is that there is no way to know what activities live in each zone for each person without knowing them well. For some students, speaking in public could be very safe, but for others, it might be incredibly dangerous. The same could be said for meeting new people, reading out loud, or tying shoelaces. Some students might have very narrow zones of risk; others might have risk zones a mile wide (see Figure 2.3). The only way to know is to ask, to pay attention, to really get to know your students. And the only way to do that is to plan carefully to use that "honeymoon" of the Knowledge/Communication and Cooperation stages in order to build Trust among your students. This is the work of your early days together—building a safe place in which students know each other well and can engage their zones of risk productively and safely.

Figure 2.3   Different Students, Different Risk Zones

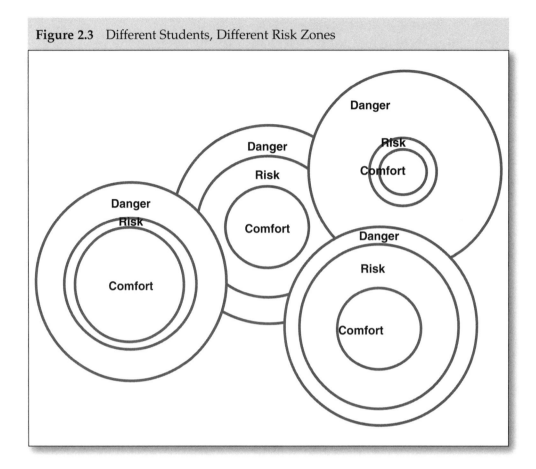

No matter the age group, building this community involves some common strategies. In fact, Knowledge/Communication is the stage in which most traditional team-building activities are useful. In most cases, this is the *only* stage in the development of the CLC in which they serve any purpose at all. Name games and activities such as Liars' Club and Personality Bingo (see the end of this chapter for more details) all provide safe ways for students to get to know one another at a most basic level. They set a personal tone in the classroom that lays the groundwork for future academic engagement.

Some elementary teachers build many of these sorts of activities into the first weeks of school, but middle and secondary teachers may feel they are unnecessary or childish. I can understand the fear that the time given over to community building is academic time lost, especially in quarter-length courses of eight or nine weeks. With mountains of curriculum to cover, we may feel that we need to start on day one with hardcore academic pursuits, leaving the get-to-know-you stuff for someone else to manage. My experience, however, has been just the opposite. In the classes in which I paid no attention to the community (even nine-week courses),

I ultimately had lower rates of student success. I have myriad theories as to why that was the case: Perhaps students felt less comfortable asking for extra help? Maybe they didn't feel that I valued them enough to make it worth their while to give my course their best effort? Perhaps I didn't know them well enough to plan lessons that matched their needs? Maybe my lack of personal connection to them led me to just care less about whether or not they passed? I'm not certain *what* the truth is, but the proof is in the pudding. Students do better when they know we're paying attention, that we care, and that we won't let them slide by. As Ted Sizer (1984/2004) wrote, "I won't threaten you but I expect much of you" (p. 227).

That said, academics and community building aren't necessarily at odds with one another. In Al Magnusson's seventh-grade science classroom at Hampton Academy, the year begins carefully. Al is aware that middle school is a risky time for young people, and he therefore shies away from activities that would make his already skittish students even more uncomfortable. This means he consciously avoids those activities that, for others, are the essence of team building! He instead chooses tasks that focus on knowledge, communication, and cooperation by first ensuring that students are comfortable in the physical space—that they know where they should sit, where they'll find the things they need, etc. On the first day, he starts them off working in teams with content—some previously learned and some new. They engage in simple activities at which they are certain to succeed. He communicates his expectations openly and asks students to share their expectations of him, but he keeps the conversation light and quick, knowing that, if necessary, he can revisit the topic later, when the students have gained trust in him and one another. Students begin to engage in Speed Grouping during the first days of school, learning basic vocabulary (along with the names and faces of their peers) in rapidly shifting groups. (See the end of this chapter for more detailed information on this activity.)

Al believes that students at this level feel safest engaging with one another when the focus is academic, that they are most comfortable using the "cover" of the task as a way to connect rather than connecting via more traditional team-building activities. This is true for many adolescents—they are safer connecting around a task than around their own unique qualities and personalities. In my first classroom, I made the mistake of asking students to begin the year by introducing a partner—sharing name, grade, and one funny or interesting thing that had happened the previous summer. The response to what I considered a fairly innocuous task was less than enthusiastic. Looking back, I can see that the environment (an unknown teacher new to the school in a class on public speaking combining all grade levels, academic tracks, and social groups) was filled with too many threats. In later years, I asked students to line up (without speaking) by the first letters of their last names, taking away the need for any verbal interaction, building on something completely neutral, and allowing me to create an immediate opportunity for success at a rather unorthodox task. (It also gave me a painless way to get through the first-day-of-class roll-call issue. Students told me their preferred, correctly pronounced first names and were spared the pain of hearing a given-but-never-used name read aloud in class.)

Jenn Huard says,

> Building trust takes time. If the teacher gives respect to students and creates an environment where students are expected to respect the teacher and each other, trust builds over time. We also try to establish norms early on and check in periodically to see how we are doing. We adjust as needed and set goals on how to improve. I also communicate with parents frequently. I try to always speak to the student before I speak with their parents about behavior or academic concerns. When we meet with parents, we try to have the student present. Students need to know that you are available to help them succeed and that you believe that they can.

For math and science teacher Louise Van Order Hodson at the Compass School in Westminster, Vermont, trust is something that must be reinforced intentionally:

> I don't let the little comments slide, but I also don't make a big deal about them. For example, if a kid calls someone a name or a project boring, I will just say, "That isn't okay," and move on without stopping the flow. This way they know I am looking out for them in more ways than just their education and they trust me to do so. I also tell them grading is about communication. If they disagree with a grade or would like to alter a grade, they can write me a note with their perspective or add more to an assignment. This way dialogue is created, and they don't feel like I am out to get them.

It is also of vital importance that you and your students clarify expectations early in your time together. This could look like the cocreation of class expectations through the drafting of a Full-Value Contract, class norms, or class expectations. (Note: My preferred language is *expectations*, but others prefer *norms* or *guidelines*. The key element, no matter what language is used, is that we create shared, public expectations determined by the

> ❝ Take the mystery out of what you expect, and you're more likely to get what you really want because most of our students *do* want to be successful. ❞

community as opposed to by the teacher alone.) By definition, a *rule* is "an authoritative, prescribed direction for conduct," but an *expectation* is "anticipation with reason or justification." Reason and justification are key—students and teachers determine what we expect and why *we* expect certain things in *our* classroom. Take the mystery out of what you expect, and you're more likely to get what you really want because most of our students *do* want to be successful.

Erin Hunter moves the students toward expectations right off the bat. In her words, "I whack 'em with the [Full-Value] Contract." She utilizes a modified Give to Get[1] process in which she asks students some basic questions:

- Why are you here?
- What do you want out of this year?
- What are you willing to give to get that?
- What do you need from each other if you're going to be successful?

Erin takes some ownership of the community as well by asking students, "What do you want from me?" and offering up what she's willing to give in order to get what she needs.

BOX 2.1   GIVE TO GET INSTRUCTIONS

Begin by posting these four questions on a chart pack (one question per chart) or on the board (in columns):

- Why are you here?
- How can I help you learn?
- What do you want to get out of this workshop (class)?
- What if you resisted learning?

Using either a Think/Pair/Share or Carousel, give students time to think, discuss, and record/report their answers. Review all answers aloud and circle or make note of those things you cannot do in the time given. Explain briefly why.

Give students a pre-prepared course content sheet or syllabus. Provide a few minutes for them to read and answer clarifying questions.

Ask participants what they are willing to give ("We'll listen quietly to instructions.") to get things they asked for in the Think/Pair/Share or Carousel

(Continued)

(Continued)

("We want to do activities instead of worksheets."), as well as all of the content you came prepared to deliver. Write their answers on large chart pack for all to see. Clarify where necessary and check that all group members can try to give these things.

Share a pre-prepared list of your "gives to get" as the teacher/facilitator.

Share nonnegotiables (e.g., "Come to class on time, participate, etc."). It is important that this nonnegotiable list not be too long.

Source: Created by Maura Hart, EdD.

"I often also include, 'What happens if you resist learning?'" Erin adds. Before finalizing an agreement, however, Erin provides many different methods for students to explore each of these ideas in different ways. For example, students may discuss each of these questions (often rephrased and reframed) in the large group or with partners or may write on them for several days before finally writing and signing a Full-Value Contract for the class. At this point, Erin finds that her students have moved into the Cooperation stage and are ready to take on more meaningful, content-based work.

Allison Robinson, social studies teacher at Monadnock Regional Middle School in Swanzey, New Hampshire, follows a similar plan, having students discuss their expectations for one another and for her as they create Classroom Policies (see Figure 2.4). Allison also challenges students to create "base teams" to serve as home groups throughout the term. These teams are students' "go-to" groups for problem-solving, sharing, and discussion, though other groups are typically utilized for longer projects and challenges (see Figure 2.5).

Figure 2.4   Classroom Policies, Group Created

1. BE RESPECTFUL
   - Show respect to staff and classmates. We do a lot of discussion and group work. Do not talk over, swear at, or insult others. Be courteous!
   - If you need to leave the room (use the bathroom, etc.), please ask at an appropriate time. You may have to wait a few minutes, but you will be able to go if there is a valid reason.
   - Use of computers and other school supplies is a privilege, so use them carefully.

2. BE PREPARED

- Come prepared for class on a daily basis. This includes bringing your homework, notebook, and, most important, something to write with.
- Turn in homework complete and *on time.* Work not turned in on time gets a zero for Homework Quality, but it will get credit for Homework Quantity.

3. BE RESPONSIBLE

- You are responsible for making up any missed work. See me as soon as possible to make up anything missed after you've been out.
- You are expected to be honest and take responsibility for your own actions, even if someone else started it. Please do not lie or make lame excuses.
- Report to class *on time.*

4. DO YOUR BEST

- If you are having a problem, talk to me. This includes problems ·with the type of work I assign or just everyday stuff. Everyone has a life outside of school, and sometimes things come up. I can be very flexible if I know what is going on.

Source: Allison Robinson. Used with permission.

Figure 2.5   Base Teams Challenge

Problem One: Dividing into Teams
Criteria:

- You must have at least one boy and one girl in each group.
- Your group must be no larger than five people and no smaller than three people.

Problem Two: Name Your Team
Criteria:

- The name must represent the whole group.
- Everyone must suggest a different name to begin with.
- The name must be agreed upon by all members.

Problem Three: Make the Poster
Content:

- a. Show who the people in the group are.

Quality Criteria for Poster:

- See handout generated by class.

Source: Allison Robinson. Used with permission.

Jennifer Huard's Academic Support Handout (Figure 2.6) allows her to lay the groundwork with her students by making clear not only her expectations but also what students can expect from the program.

Figure 2.6 Academic Support

Goals of Academic Support:
- To work on goals and objectives and to monitor skill progress
- To receive assistance with the completion of attempted homework
- To receive assistance in organizing, managing time, prioritizing workload, and developing study skills
- To address academic challenges and develop strategies
- To have an opportunity for reteaching of concepts

What I expect from you:
- Agendas should be opened when you arrive to Academic Support so they can be checked.
- All students are expected to work productively through the entire Academic Support period and are expected to document work completed on a daily basis.
- You should bring "reading for enjoyment" books or magazines to class *every day* to read in case you don't have any work.
- iPods can be used only if permission has been given and only if you have handed in all of your homework on time.
- Once a week, we will devote time to organizing our notebooks, binders, and sometimes our backpacks.
- Specific skill-building activities and progress monitoring will occur for either part of or the entire class period once or twice a week. This takes precedence over all schoolwork.

What you can expect from the teacher:
- I hold high expectations for my students. You are all bright and capable! I will work really hard to provide assistance and teach you strategies, skills, and core content material. In return, I expect that you will try your hardest.
- I expect students to respect each other as well. Academic Support is not a free period for socializing. Assigned seats will be given if needed. If a student continues to be disruptive after I have spoken to him or her twice, that student will be asked to leave the classroom and will make up missed up time with me at another time.
- I communicate home frequently about grades, upcoming tests and assignments, and work completion. If you have been missing assignments or grades are slipping, I will contact your parents/guardian.
- I will help you find out about your learning style and needs and help you learn to use strategies to be successful in school and in life.
- I communicate daily with all of the team teachers. I work on designing curriculum, lessons, and tests and quizzes. I help the teachers meet the needs of all of their students.

Grading:
- Academic Support is a Pass or No Credit class that is an elective credit. If you are productive in Academic Support more than 70 percent of the time, you will pass. If you are not productive doing schoolwork and working on goals, objectives, and organization at least 70 percent of the time, you will receive a No Credit for the course.

- Effort grades are given to reflect how much effort you put into class. Effort grades are as follows:

  1. **Needs Improvement.** Frequent redirection needed daily to stay on task and student is productive less than 70 percent of the time (less than 35 minutes).

  2. **Approaches Expectations.** Student needs three to five cues to stay on task and is productive most of the class (about 80 percent or 40 minutes).

  3. **Meets Expectations.** Student works hard for at least 90 percent of the class (45 minutes) and requires no more than two reminders to stay on task.

  4. **Exceeds Expectations.** Student works diligently throughout the class.

_____   _____
Student Signature   Date

_____   _____
Parent Signature   Date

_____   _____
Teacher Signature   Date

Source: Jenn Huard, Learning Specialist. Used with permission.

There are a plethora of team-building activities out there, and everyone has his or her favorites. If you find that don't have favorites—or any ideas at all—see the Appendix of this book for some great resources. In the meantime here are few activities that you might try:

- **Personality Bingo/Scavenger Hunt.** Using basic information shared by students (or information so ubiquitous as to be certain to include all students), create a bingo card with descriptors of members of the class (e.g., "loves to read," "hates sports," "was born in this town," "has moved more than once," "owns a car"). Students who embody that characteristic sign next to the descriptor. The winner is the student who fills his card first.

- **I Like People Who.** Create a circle of chairs with one fewer chair than you have people in the room. (The teacher plays, so don't forget to count yourself!) As students take their seats, ask them to begin by thinking of things about themselves that they think others will share in common. The teacher begins by saying, "I like people who . . ." and then states a fact about herself. Anyone who has that fact in common with the speaker rises and switches chairs with the other people who have risen (the teacher now takes a chair as well). The last person left without a chair then says, "I like people who . . . ," and the game continues.

- **People to People.** The teacher should create a list of questions such as "What is your favorite kind of pizza? What is your favorite/ least favorite class? What is your favorite band/kind of music? What was the last movie you saw? What kind of books do you like to read?" Students are then asked to quickly (never taking more than two minutes) group themselves by their responses to these questions. You may find that you need to tell students where to group themselves—in the corners of the room, for example—or you may choose not to provide any information about how the grouping should take place. You may also find that you need to ask students to do it silently or in whispers because the noise level can get intense with this activity. (Note: Types of questions can be modified —"My group needed more ____ on this project," or "If I were going to do this project over, I'd be sure to ____"— to make this an interesting debriefing activity as well.)

- **Line Up (aka Last Name Lineup).** Offer the following instructions: "Without speaking or writing, please line up by the first letter of your last name. If necessary, alphabetize within letters as well: Singh comes after Sanchez but before Southwick." You may choose to offer additional scaffolding by designating the beginning and end of the line. This activity can be modified by asking students to line up by birthdays or by their opinions on various topics (e.g., "Line up by how much you like football, by how much you know about *Romeo and Juliet,* by how well you understand the process of mitosis, by how much you agree that the New Deal was a good idea").

- **Liars' Club (aka "Two Truths and a Lie").** This is a good basic community-building activity that can be adapted easily for reflection. It can be done as a whole group or with smaller groups of three to five students. Individually, each student must make three statements, one of which is untrue. The group then must decide together which of the three is the lie. Each student takes a turn until everyone has shared.

- **Speed Grouping/Pinwheels.** Create two circles with the same number of chairs, one within the other, the inner facing the outer. (Students seated in the inner circle will remain stationary throughout the activity.) The teacher should pose a question and give students a brief period (two to three minutes) for discussion, then ask the outer circle to move one seat clockwise. The teacher may then repeat the question or pose a new prompt for discussion.

Moving beyond the first three stages of building a CLC (Knowledge/Communication, Cooperation, and Trust) requires both patience and a willingness to challenge the group. You must be willing not only to watch and wait, observing your students (Who talks? Who doesn't? Who emerges as a leader? Who follows whom? Which students take a "wait and see" approach?) in order to better anticipate their responses in future situations but also to use this new knowledge to create opportunities for them to engage (with the content and with one another) in ways that may be less traditional in a classroom setting. Ultimately, building community is best done through the meaningful work of curriculum-based problem solving—but that will come later in your time together. In these earliest days, students must build trust in one another—and in you—in order to be willing to engage in that work. If they

> 66 Ultimately, building community is best done through the meaningful work of curriculum-based problem solving. 99

are to trust you with their best selves, they must know that you—and their peers—will welcome and support their efforts. It is actually that trust that will serve as a bridge over the conflict that marks the end of the "honeymoon" and the beginning of real engagement: the Collaboration and Maturation/Maintenance stages.

While the first three stages of the CLC's development require specific, intentional attention to the CLC itself, the last two (and more powerful) stages require a shift from the CLC as the primary focus, with the curriculum acting in its service, to the content as the focus with the CLC acting in its service. Quite simply, the last two stages are about the shift from "learning how to be a community" to "using the community to learn." In order to do this, you have to create real, meaningful, content-rich experiences driven by contextual, engaging experiences rooted in explicit content and process standards. These meaningful learning experiences are the fodder—and the reward—for the work of shifting your instructional practice. In the next chapter, I'll show you how to begin to reimagine instruction and put your CLC to work by first gaining clarity about what you expect from your students in terms of their behavior and the content you're teaching.

NOTE

1. Give to Get © Maura Hart, EdD. Used with permission.

3

Aiming

Gaining Clarity

To have an aim is to act with meaning.

—John Dewey, *Democracy and Education,* 1916

Now that you've done the early work of building and maintaining a collaborative learning community, how do you make that CLC work for you? How do you move into the curriculum and reap the reward of higher student achievement and engagement? The framework for Next Generation instruction is the next step in your movement toward more effective pedagogy.

Remember, Next Generation instruction moves students out of a passive role where learning is concerned. It both requires and supports full participation, making the community authentic and vital to students' day-to-day experience. Next Generation instruction is rooted in inquiry, in the experiential cycle (see Kolb, 1984), and builds on a simple foundation.

To review, Next Generation instructors do the following:

- Plan experiences rooted in big questions, themes, and connections with clearly defined expectations for success in content, form, and process.

- Engage students in the work by "giving them the keys," providing resources, and then observing and supporting and guiding their efforts through questioning and—most important—staying out of the way.
- Debrief the experience to help codify new content and process knowledge. Provide feedback on what they saw and heard but, more important, ask questions about what students saw and heard and help them to draw connections between their observations and expectations (McGrath, 2007).

BOX 3.1   RESOURCES FOR PLANNING INSTRUCTION

While the purpose of this book is to help you re-imagine the way you work with your students, it is firmly rooted in the facilitation and coaching portions of the transition and can't possibly serve as an exhaustive compendium on both this and planning experiential, inquiry-based lessons. For more on that subject, I recommend the following organizations and their publications:

Antioch University–New England–Critical Skills Program, www.antiochne.edu/acsr/criticalskills/

Coalition of Essential Schools, www.essentialschools.org

Buck Institute for Education, www.bie.org

George Lucas Educational Foundation/Edutopia, www.edutopia.org

International Baccalaureate, www.ibo.org

National Service-Learning Clearinghouse, www.servicelearning.org

QED Foundation, www.qedfoundation.org

THE FRAMEWORK FOR NEXT GENERATION INSTRUCTIONAL FACILITATION

Facilitation (as opposed to instruction) requires us to shift our perspective from that of a "deliverer of educational services" to that of a more student-centered "creator and manager of learning experiences." As mentioned above, learning is done by the learner, and while the teacher's shift away from center stage can feel awkward at first, with time and experience you'll come to appreciate the power of this new way of teaching and learning. The elements of the framework[1] are easy to remember:

- Aiming
- Framing
- Gaming
- Claiming
- Exclaiming

Aiming

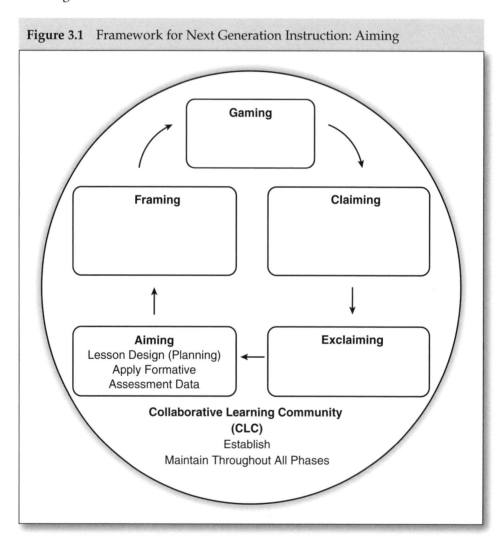

Figure 3.1   Framework for Next Generation Instruction: Aiming

In the aiming phase of the Next Generation instruction framework, we gather information, and we plan for content and process learning. The work you do in building (and maintaining) your CLC is the foundation of your Aiming phase—it will help you to know and adjust for not only the evolving maturity and developmental levels, characteristics, and objectives of your students but also their changing interests, passions, and fears. In Aiming—planning for specific lessons—you'll need to not only

> 66 The most important element here is *clarity*. If you are clear about what you want from your students, you are much more likely to get it. 99

review the specific learning (content) and process (skills/dispositions) goals, activities, and tools you plan to use in a single day but also look across the scope of the unit. The most important element here is *clarity*. If you are clear about what you want from your students, you are much more likely to get it.

Quinn's six questions[2] can help you gain clarity around both content and process:

1. **What am I teaching?** What are the content standards and the skills/dispositions/habits/behaviors my students need to know and demonstrate at the culmination of this unit or lesson?

2. **Why am I teaching it?** What use is this content to my students?

3. **How am I teaching it?** Is this an opportunity for a service-learning project? An inquiry-driven unit? What role, if any, can technology play? How can I shift the responsibility for learning—the hard work—onto the students? What is going on in the community or the world that connects to this?

4. **Why am I teaching it that way?** Is this simply the way I learned it? The way the others in my department teach it? Is it connected to a district/state mandate or initiative?

5. **How do I know my kids are getting it?** What concrete, observable behaviors and products will be demonstrated and created? How will I know if students have done the work and done it well? By what criteria will I evaluate student work?

6. **How do the kids know they are getting it?** What reflective techniques will I use to help the students assess their own learning? How can I be sure they understand what they're learning and how they can use it in the future?

In Erin Hunter's carpentry classroom, Aiming looks different depending on the lesson, the students, and the time of year. In her words, "the first [lesson] will look different from the 4th to the 20th." For instance, her second activity depends largely on how the first activity was handled by the students. As a reflective practitioner, she gathers formative data in order to Aim for the next lesson. The first assignment—an exploration of the hand tools available to students—is mirrored in the second—an exploration of the power tools.

> [The power tool problem] is usually only the second time they've done anything like this. The two are very similar in their structure and the content that is required—identification of the tool, what it's used for, how you safely use it and maintain it. There's the intentionality in that, though, because they inevitably in the first [activity] assume you want them to make a poster. Everyone looks at everyone else, and everyone is making a poster. Keep in mind, this is a lab *full* of hand tools. I don't say, "Make a poster." I deliberately do not tell them what I want for a product—they just have to make a presentation to the class—but still, they make the poster because it's just so ingrained in their school lives.
>
> Now, I'm trying to touch on multiple areas here—the power tool identification as well as their mental horizons for how they best demonstrate what they have learned and know. I deliberately word the power tool challenge so it is more open ended—so the product is more ambiguous. I say, "You need to present to the boss. Your company is expanding, and you're going to be a crew out on your own. Your boss has asked you to come up with a collection of power tools you need. He doesn't want to spend a lot of money unless he knows that you know how to use and maintain them safely. You'll need to present: What tools you need, what you'll use them for, the approximate cost, and how you'll use and maintain them safely." Sometimes I add that they'll need to produce a hard-copy list. Inevitably, out come the posters.
>
> Now, the first question from them should be (but never is) "What kind of jobs will we be doing for this new division of the company?" By the second challenge, they *ask that question*—because the end of the first challenge leads them to the question. I also make sure that they get that the posters are totally irrelevant to the challenge. We get to that in the debriefing.

The main structure of the lesson doesn't change from class to class, but Erin may rethink the ways she connects the first and second challenge, the level of correction and direction she offers, the level of reassurance and cheerleading necessary, and the grouping mechanism and the parameters for the presentation.

The Otter Valley High School Ninth-Grade Team (Caitlin Steele, Chris Lemieux, and Bruce Perlow) says,

> We plan collaboratively. Often we brainstorm together, one person drafts a lesson/unit, and then we workshop and revise it together. We each bring different skills and experiences to the table, so each

has different insight into what would work well and better for students. Together, we set realistic expectations for the number of sources or notecards students would need, for example, and how much time to provide for particular steps. We draw on our collective experience to consider potential pitfalls before presenting a lesson and use student successes, struggles, and feedback to reflect and revise after the fact. Lessons, projects, and units are designed around essential and guiding questions, so we provide a standards-based framework for projects.

For a special educator like Jenn Huard working across multiple classrooms, the process is different but still rooted in clarity.

I need to know what the objective and goal of the lesson is. Using the S-M-A-R-T-E-R (Specific, Measurable, Achievable, Realistic, Time Sensitive, Emotionally Resonant) method along with Understanding by Design will help to ensure that the lesson is student centered. It is important to evaluate lessons from class to class and year to year as needs of the class change as the students change. It is important to evaluate whether a lesson would be engaging to students and to collect some data using a pre-assessment and your knowledge of the students to ensure that you are meeting students where they are currently at. Assuming all students are competent is essential.

Math and science teacher Louise Van Order Hodson starts with Howard Gardner's theory of multiple intelligences, asking herself, "Where is the creative side of this lesson? When will we be up and active? What kids will excel at this?"

Allison Robinson, a middle school social studies teacher at Monadnock Regional Middle/High School in Swanzey, New Hampshire, focuses on questions like these:

What are the essential pieces of knowledge that I need them to leave the lesson with? What are the skills I want them to get from this? What information/skills do they need to already have to get this new essential knowledge? How can I get them to "find/discover" the essential knowledge on their own? How can I make this fun for a seventh grader? What are their interests—what is their motivation? What have I got for resources?"

Technology integration specialist Dan Callahan notes that teachers are often creatures of habit and that shaking up the end product can help them reconnect to their instructional goals.

The big issue I run into is that people are really attached to a specific project—the books, the speeches, the dioramas. They don't worry as much about the process by which they arrive at the product, and the content gets lost. What are different ways that we could meet the actual instructional goals? Forget about previous products. What are the goals, and what are different ways to meet them? For some teachers, the "project-y" place is a place to start introducing the tech tools.

If you're one of those teachers who could stand to use more technology in your instruction, perhaps looking at your favorite projects would be a good place to start.

As you plan, think carefully about what you know about your students—about their capacity to manage frustration, their experiences with problem solving, and their prior knowledge of the content and the resources available to them. Then create a situation in which just one or two of these elements are more challenging.

If your students typically spend their days filling out worksheets on which the answers can be found in a word bank at the top of the page, then don't expect them to be terribly creative problem solvers right off the bat. To help them transition to a more facilitative method of learning, structure a lesson in which the answers can be found in a short reading you provide; then perhaps in three readings provided to them; then perhaps in a carefully selected set of mixed materials provided to the class as a whole, available on a resource table. If they typically work alone, don't assign them a group task until they first spend time practicing, perhaps with assigned roles with clear, concrete, observable expectations for each person in the group. For example, "The recorder writes, but he can't talk," can be a useful instruction if you want to be sure the recorder doesn't just do the work for the group, as can "The recorder can only write down what other people say." The facilitator could be tasked with making sure that everyone in the group takes a turn speaking. The materials person is in charge of getting whatever the group may need and ensures that everything gets returned at the end—including the finished work. The messenger is the only one who can ask questions of the teacher or of other groups.

Those experienced with cooperative learning will find these roles familiar and easy to assign. If you're unfamiliar with the use of roles, consider the task at hand and the jobs that need to be done in order to complete it successfully. Define and divide these jobs into simple job titles, and then let the number of jobs determine the size of each group. Post each job and its associated responsibilities where everyone can see them and provide an easy way to identify which person has which job. Typical roles might include the following:

- Facilitator/Leader
- Recorder/Writer

- Getter/Errand runner
- Questioner/Presenter
- Timekeeper
- Checker
- Process observer

For more information on this topic, you might want to check out *The Teacher's Sourcebook for Cooperative Learning: Practical Techniques, Basic Principles, and Frequently Asked Questions* by Jacobs, Power, and Loh (2002).

NOTES

1. American Youth Foundation, 1997. Used with permission.
2. Quinn, n.d. Used with permission.

4

Framing and Gaming

Games lubricate the body and the mind.

—Benjamin Franklin

FRAMING

Framing is the first experience that your students will have with the lesson. It is your opening gambit, your hook. Frame the lesson through its connection to your students. Use your technology to bring the larger context into your classroom. Answer the eternal question "Why *do* they need to learn this stuff?" This will give you points of reference to return to and a modicum of credibility from your students' point of view. Focus your students at the outset on both the learning and the process objectives—both what they'll show they know and how they'll show it. Review your Full Value Contract/Classroom Expectations to remind everyone of the expectations to support the community. Restate the learning objectives frequently and give clear instructions both verbally and in posted, written form (via the board or chart pack). Make sure students understand what they are supposed to do and what limits they need to be aware of, as well as any other considerations such as resource limits and availability, time frames, etc. Don't assume that they know just because you told them: "Chunk" the problem or task with them, asking them to break the work down into steps and elements, which they then

Figure 4.1   Framework for Next Generation Instruction: Framing

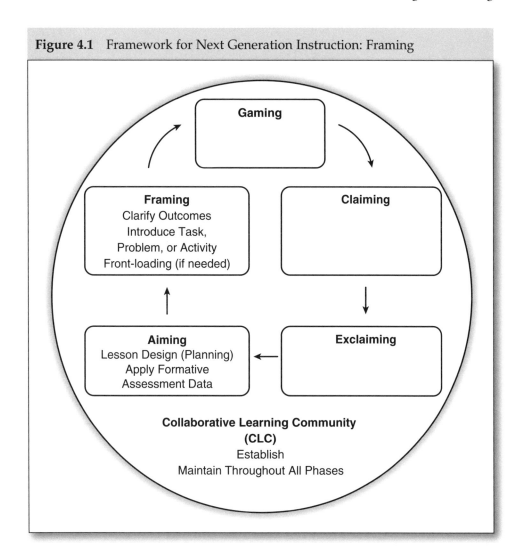

report back to you. Depending on the group's level of skill and your own comfort level, you might ask:

- What will you produce?
- When will it be finished?
- What time/day do you need to be done?
- What steps will you take in getting this done?
- What do you want to make sure you do/don't do while you're working on this?
- How will you know when you're done?
- What are you trying to show that you know?

As middle school teacher Al Magnusson says,

BOX 4.1   FRONTLOADING

In the experiential learning community, the term *frontloading* is often used to describe activities and instruction provided to students in the Framing stage before they begin a new task. Frontloading serves the following purposes:

- Revisit past commitments, goals, and content knowledge.
  "At the end of your last speech, you set some goals about what you were going to do differently next time. Please share those goals with the group one more time before we start."
- Preview future content or process learning.
  "What do you think the class will get out of doing this activity? What do you think this unit is designed to teach? Why are we doing this?"
- Make connections between the new task or skill and real-world applications.
  "Where might this learning be useful in your life outside of school? In your other classes?"
- Review positive experiences and knowledge that may be applicable to the new task.
  "What will the group need to do in order to succeed? What strategies can the group use to make sure these things happen? What did we do last time that worked for us? How can we apply that to this problem?"
- Review negative experiences that students will wish to avoid.
  "What things has this group done in the past that may get in the way? What can the group do to make sure these don't happen this time? What did we do last time that prevented us from being as successful as we could have been? What should we do differently this time? How can we apply that to this problem?"

One caution, however: Frontloading can easily become an excuse to give students information that they could discover easily—and more meaningfully—on their own. For example, you may be tempted to review (or introduce) vocabulary before students begin a unit. It will be more meaningful, however, if students must define terms as necessary, in the moment that they realize (and perhaps ask you), "I don't know what this means. What does it mean?" The best answer in that moment is "Well, where you could you find out?" followed by a smile.

I think Framing has to be very well thought out. One time early in my career I showed my classes an exemplary final project. This project was the best one from the previous year's students who'd done the same project. I even hung it up at the front of the class. The students did a great job with the project, except for one thing . . . all the projects looked practically identical to the one I showed them. Another time the students were sort of stuck on what to sketch for their earth science unit portfolio graphic, and I said, "Oh, whatever is good. You know, like a volcano or something." That was all it took, and almost all of them drew volcanoes. I think it's crucial to show exemplary work; just vary the examples from the project the students will work on. I also make sure I wean them away from being shown examples as quickly as possible, so they can define quality work for themselves.

Middle school teacher Allison Robinson starts by giving her students a written version of the assignment—either one per group or one per person—outlining the project. Students work in groups to "chunk" the challenge, taking it apart to determine what it requires in terms of process, form, and content. They then report out to the whole class, building a shared understanding of the task, resources, and expectations. She's arranged her classroom to make this simpler: "I have tables in my classroom. They were something I asked for once I started using these methods more because it made group work easier."

The team from Otter Valley uses a similar process:

Big projects were always presented first by the whole team of teachers to the whole group of students so that everyone was on the same page starting off. After presenting the entire piece, we would take questions for clarification and further explanation, and we would clarify the "next step" before setting the students free to get started. Throughout the process, we did a lot of circulating to make sure everyone was heading in the right direction. Generally, we would make a point of regrouping the next day to touch base, field further questions, reinforce, and/or redirect based on observations, conversations with students, their questions, frustrations, and feedback.

Learning specialist Jenn Huard says,

First and foremost, you need to engage the students by presenting a problem that is high interest or that they can have personal connection with. It is vital that students know what the goal of the activity is. The teacher should always provide instructions orally and in written format. I prefer students have them not only written on the board but in a checklist form as well so they can be sure that they have all required components and can easily refer to them. This is very helpful for students who have executive functioning difficulties. Additionally, many students may benefit from being shown how to use the checklist and other metacognitive strategies such as evaluating their performance as they go. The teacher can model this by talking aloud, showing metacognition strategies.

Once students are working, teachers need to check in on students to be sure they are on the right track. We all know the students *who don't know that they don't know,* so it is important that we catch those students and groups quickly. It is more difficult to unlearn and correct than it is to learn it correctly with some extra support in the first place. For example, if a student believes that all angles in a triangle add up to 360 degrees and quickly works through a packet solving all problems based on that belief, it will be very difficult for that student to unlearn that and correct it to know that all triangles equal 180 degrees.

Framing can be fun—even silly—and can build the CLC by becoming part of the identity of the course. For example, Allison's fictional and very spirited Great Aunt Mildred provides a consistent character whose requests and adventures create fodder for challenges throughout her course.

BOX 4.2

Great Aunt Mildred's U.S. Road Trip

My Great Aunt Mildred had always wanted to see all 50 states, but now that she is in a nursing home, she can no longer travel. She has given you and your group three in-class days plus the long weekend to put together an information packet about your randomly chosen state to share with her and the rest of the residents of her nursing home. She expects that the packets will be neatly organized and constructed as well as use a variety of colors to keep the elderly patients interested.

Using the following graphs:

- Bar graph
- Line graph
- Pictograph
- Climagraph
- Circle graph
- Table
- Timeline
- Montage

Graph the following information:

- Temperature and precipitation for the state capital for every month of the year
- 10 important events in the state's history
- Population of 10 cities or towns in the state
- 5 interesting (or strange) landmarks/ places to visit in the state
- The 5 longest rivers, highest points, or deepest lakes in the state
- The percentage of major ethnic groups in the state's population
- The total state population over the past 50 years
- 5 facts about the state as compared to two other states

You must graph all the information on the right using all of the graphs on the left once. You will need to decide which graph will be the best to use when graphing each kind of information. To get the information, you will need to use books, almanacs, and the Internet and make sure that you cite the source(s) of your information on your graph.

Great Aunt Mildred's Space Shot

My eccentric Great Aunt Mildred is at it again. As a young woman, she had always wanted to go someplace no one had ever been before. In today's world, it is difficult to find uncharted land on Earth, given the extent to which people have traveled the world. To find a place where no one has ever been before, we need to look to space. Surprisingly, she has met a man in the nursing home who happens to own a rocket ship, and she has negotiated for your team to use the ship to travel to an uncharted land, on an uncharted planet, in an uncharted solar system to give you the opportunity to do what she was never able to do. (With all that "uncharted," you might wonder how she knows you'll get there?) Unfortunately the ship is very small and can hold only your team and supplies of food and oxygen for three days.

In return for funding your trip, Great Aunt Mildred and her gentleman friend would like your team to send the maps of the now-charted land to them so that they can share it with their friends at the nursing home. They would like to see a physical, a political, and a special-purpose map, and although they do not expect it, a contour map would be a useful addition. Great Aunt Mildred would also like a letter from each of you that reflects on the experience of your trip, including the research process and the map-creating experience. Since you will not be at the nursing home to explain your maps to the residents, your maps should stand on their own and be easy for people to figure out.

Before going on your trip, we will set up a rubric to evaluate whether your maps include all the parts of a map and how well you illustrated the type of map you were suppose to create.

Although each of you is responsible for putting forth your best effort, you might want to take on different roles each day to keep the project moving.

Source: Allison Robinson. Used with permission.

Math and science teacher Louise Van Order Hodson begins by showing a sample product related to the assignment and having the students grade it. "This way," she says, "they are familiar with the rubric and with the expectations. I have gotten far better results this way." For technology integration specialist Dan Callahan, Framing is an excellent place to integrate technology. For example, one might use an interactive whiteboard to work with a social network site like Twitter, a wiki, or a

YouTube video to pull students into the lesson; help them understand what they need to do; and engage them in a meaningful process. As another example, a Skype call from a geographically distant expert who explains why students need to collect data or oral histories, followed by a report about using the same technology, can connect students to their work more powerfully than making a presentation to their peers ever could.

Al Magnusson says,

> To develop kids as thinkers, we have to allow our Framing to have elements of open-endedness. In my science classroom, many times I will try to do a demonstration that is related to the self-directed work they are going to do. This demonstration can have some unique quality to it, an anomaly. This makes for a great hook. I create the "need to know," the mystery for the students. The idea that they are going to figure something out sets up a wonderful platform for them to start their inquiry. The culture of the classroom has established patterns of how we proceed with certain types of assignments. Once this culture gets fairly well set up, I tend to see if the students themselves can "run" the beginning of these different types of assignments. At that point, we examine what leadership looks and sounds like. The students are invested into the whole process. As the "guide," I will always be cognizant of their process and interject help at any point if they stray too far from the objectives. I might reference questions like . . .
>
> • What are trying to do right now?
> • What are you trying to create?
> • What does the assignment ask you to show/ make/figure out?
> • What do you think you need to do next?
> • What's your plan? How's it working?
>
> . . . to give the class guidance to get back on track. It's important to recognize that this level of methodology takes time for the kids as well as the teacher. I think it's also important for the teacher to have some experience with the curriculum—it's hard to facilitate if you don't know the content very well.

In Aiming and Framing, teachers must be careful to target the instructional "sweet spot" at which the activity is messy enough to be challenging but not so messy as to be too frustratingly difficult. Remember, your students' capacities to solve ill-defined problems must be developed, particularly if they haven't used them much before.

A problem such as one of the Aunt Mildred Challenges can be overwhelming to beginners. An appropriate decline of the level of scaffolding might sound like this:

1. Everything you need to finish this project is in the paragraph at the bottom of the page.

2. Everything you need to solve this problem is in the attached handout.

3. Everything you need to figure this out is on the table by the window.

4. Everything you need to do this can be found in this room.

5. Everything you need to know or have can be found in this room or the library.

6. You can utilize any resources you can think of and access to get this done.

For example, Allison Robinson's scaffolds her Religion Poster assignment through the use of clarifying questions and carefully selected resources.

BOX 4.3   RELIGION POSTER

Goal: To create a poster that shows people what your assigned religion is all about. Each person in the group will be assigned a piece of the religion picture. Each individual is responsible for his or her piece and getting that piece onto the poster. You will want to coordinate the placement of each piece of the religion picture.

_____ **Sacred Places** (geographic places of particular spiritual significance)
- Where is it? (Describe its relative location—what is it close to; next to; near; north, south, east, or west of?)
- Find a map of where that place or those places are.

_____ **Sacred Spaces** (places of worship)
- What are they called? (Is there more than one?)
- What do they look like? (Are there different varieties?)
- Where are they located?
- Find a picture of an example.

_____ **Sacred Symbols**
- What symbols are important?
- What do they mean?

(Continued)

(Continued)

- Why are they important?
- Find a picture of the symbol(s).

_____ **Sacred Holidays**

- For some religions there might be many . . . choose at least two of the most important.
- When is it celebrated?
- Why do they celebrate it?
- Find a picture of a celebration.

_____ **Sacred Texts or Holy Books**

- What is the name of the book(s)?
- What basic information is contained in them?
- Find a picture of one.

_____ **Guides or Codes of Behavior**

- What are the major "rules" of the religion?

_____ **Specific Religious or Spiritual Leaders**

- Who are the founders of the religion?
- What is their history?
- In the present day, who are the people who lead others in the religion? (priest, rabbi, imam, lama, etc.)
- What qualifications must leaders have?
- Find an image of one.

Some Sources You Can Use:

http://www.uri.org/kids/world.htm

http://www.religionfacts.com/big_religion_chart.htm

http://www.religionfacts.com/a-z-religion-index/index.htm

http://library.thinkquest.org/28505/

http://library.thinkquest.org/J002592/

http://wri.leaderu.com/wri-table2/table2.html

Source: Allison Robinson. Used with permission.

Aiming and Framing are largely the work of the teacher. They are the stages in which you gain clarity about what you want your students to know and show and how they're going to do it. Careful planning at this stage will make the rest of your work simpler, if not easier. The shift from Framing to Gaming is the shift of the learning load from the teacher to the students. As stated in the *Critical Skills Level I Coaching Kit,*

> In general, if there are specific outcomes you're seeking, it helps to clearly state them. Whether it be curricular content, practice with an academic skill such as writing or speaking, or attention to a specific process skill, the best way to assure that it is addressed is to design it into the challenge. (McGrath, 2007)

In Al's Ford Motor Company Challenge (see Box 4.4), he has not only created an engaging scenario for students but also clearly articulated a problem to solve (trucks carrying heavy loads are having trouble accelerating) and a method for doing so (create an experiment demonstrating how mass/weight affect acceleration). The students are also given a clear description of what the product will look like when it's done well (proper calculations, data table, graph, an presentation, a conclusion statement, etc.) and the attributes they need to demonstrate while they're working. According to the *Critical Skills Level I Coaching Kit,*

> In this assignment, Al lists all that is required from the students. Sometimes, novice teachers overemphasize student ownership and ask them to identify what they are expected to do, how they want to exhibit their learning, and what assessment criteria should be applied to their work. While this may be honorable, if done too quickly, it may get in the way of quality learning or become an obstacle to results the teacher expects. Remember, if students fall short of expectations, it can become a wonderful learning opportunity. Through debrief or reflection students can see clearly how they can do better next time.
>
> This challenge also uses a standard mechanism for individual accountability—that of a journal entry. These kinds of individual assignments (journals, lab books, tests, essays, etc.) are ways to check for individual understanding.
>
> Individual accountability is often missing in many group work situations—sometimes hiding the fact that a single group member did the bulk of the work. An injustice is often perceived by productive students, especially if the same credit is given to those who did little. Moreover, lack of individual accountability ill serves all students who fail to learn the skills and knowledge desired from the experience. Finally, making journal entries allows students the opportunity to reflect on a more personal level. This works well for many students. The challenge refers students back to criteria that they have been using and developing for a quality presentation. For most content and skill outcomes, the characteristics of quality remain consistent from one challenge to the next.

Good posters, good decision making, and good collaboration have the same traits in many contexts. A nice way to make connections between experiences is to retain lists of assessment criteria and simply add to or modify them when you revisit a previous outcome area or product. Students are able to build on their previous work and demonstrate their increasing sophistication with recognizing quality work in whatever area you are addressing. (McGrath, 2007)

BOX 4.4   FORD MOTOR COMPANY CHALLENGE

DATE: October/November 1928
TO: Mr. Magnusson's Science Class
FROM: Board of Trustees, Ford Motor Company
RE: Ford Truck Problem

Dear Engineering Team,

As you know, since 1900 the automobile and motor truck industry has grown tremendously. Much of this is due to the vision of our founder, Henry Ford. Mr. Ford is getting many survey responses from companies indicating a problem with Ford motor trucks. It seems that motor trucks that carry heavy loads are having difficulties picking up speed on the highway. Your engineering team's challenge is to design an experiment that will demonstrate how mass/weight affects acceleration. Mr. Ford would like you to present your data findings in three days to the Ford Motor Co. trustee directors. The following is a list of requirements needed to complete this challenge. Please present the following, with excellent quality:

- An experiment with proper use of equations and calculations of acceleration with relation to mass/weight
- Data table with 0–9 trials
- Graph of data that shows how mass affects acceleration
- Presentation in a format of your choosing that explains the experiment your team performed (the presentation should demonstrate your team understands 3–5 historical event characteristics from 1900 to 1928)
- Conclusion statements about how mass affects acceleration
- Recommendations based on data analysis for what we should do with our Ford Motor Trucks.

This task is much too complex to be done by one person in such a short amount of time; hence, you must delegate work thoughtfully to all members of your team. An action plan must be submitted before research and experiments begin that details the responsibilities of each member of your group, your experimental design, and anticipated results.

As part of the overall Ford Engineering Community, it is vital that you share equipment and respect differences in others as they attempt to help the team solve this problem. It is also very important to be responsible for your individual part(s) of this task to make the project a total success for your specific team.

In addition, you must develop a system in your group for internal quality control: finding a way to get feedback within your group and improving your work based on the ideas of others.

With your Chief Project Engineer, Mr. Magnusson, design a checklist that will help you make observations of how your team is working together. Mr. Magnusson will help with deciding how frequently this checklist will be put to use. Your team should also revisit the criteria for an excellent quality presentation.

The day after presentations, a journal entry in your Ford Motor Company log book will help show if you understand how mass/weight affects acceleration and how you built on the ideas of each other in your group to produce the highest-quality products.

Source: McGrath, 2007. Used with permission.

GAMING

The bulk of your students' time will be spent in Gaming. Don't let the mnemonic device fool you—this "gaming" is serious business. This play is where the work of creating, collaborating, asking, and processing—in short, the work of learning—takes place. So you've crafted an experience for your students: a problem to solve, a question to answer, a task to complete. You've made careful decisions about what resources you want them to use and what skills you want them to practice. You've made sure they understand not only what they need to produce but what they need to show they know and can do. It's the moment to turn it over to them, to give them the keys. You've posed the problem or task, and you've helped the students clarify what they need to create, what they're supposed to demonstrate, and what roles they should be playing. They're staring at you. You're staring at them. There's a single moment of calm, and then the questions begin: "Wait. What are we supposed to do again? Where are the materials? Can I go to the library? Where is the construction paper?"

So what do you do now?

Many beginning (and experienced) facilitators struggle at this point, either with boredom or with an insatiable urge to get in the middle of the work. The wise facilitator will take this time to just pay attention. The wise educator knows that the best advice at this point is to do

Figure 4.2   Framework for Next Generation Instruction: Gaming

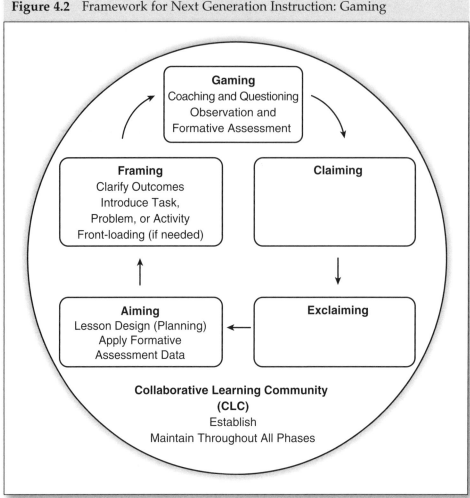

nothing. Don't do anything—just stand there. Watch for the things you said you wanted to see your students demonstrate. Make notes, ask questions, take pictures or video for use in debriefing, and just watch.

Allison notes,

> ❝ I don't hover—I'm not over their shoulders. I'm letting them move through the collaborative process. I have to remind myself to trust the process.—Al Magnusson ❞

I ask *a lot* of questions to individuals and groups while they're working: "Where are we at? What do we know? What do we still need to do/understand/know?" I don't always allow the same person from the group to answer the question. I will often call for a break in the action to check for clarity and ask more questions.

Al adds,

> I'm always taking mental snapshots of what's going on at that
> given moment. You have to have a sense of what needs to happen
> at the beginning versus later in terms of the way kids are getting
> along, what you want to see the group or the individual demon-
> strating. Early on, you have to watch every single group to see if
> they're getting through the "groping" stage, if they're figuring out
> what they need to do. Later, you're looking for something more
> than just "are they doing what I asked them to?" You're looking
> for signs that they're collaborating, not just cooperating.
>
> I think that kids are working together more than they used to.
> They're getting lots of practice at cooperating, so it's appropriate
> to expect more from them. I'm looking to see if I need to step in
> and do more coaching—to get the kids over a tough spot or a per-
> sonality issue. I may be deciding if I need to reshuffle the group or
> reframe the task. In the beginning, I'm just getting them through
> the introductory time—knowledge/communication and trust
> stages. Once they get more familiar with this, I'm trying to be a fly
> on the wall. I don't hover—I'm not over their shoulders. I'm let-
> ting them move through the collaborative process.
>
> I have to remind myself to trust the process. I'm watching to
> see if they're looking at the expectations, the rubric, the checklist
> if I gave them one. I might walk by and just point to the page
> where they can find the answer to their question or the solution
> to the problem their facing. Once they're really moving and
> working along, then I relax a bit—until they're putting together
> the final piece. Then I'm asking a question here or there: "Is that
> the direction you want to go? Is that one of the expectations? Are
> you sure about that?" I slip them little notes to encourage or cel-
> ebrate if it's going well. (Sticky notes are great for this.) I may
> give one to an individual kid if he or she asks a good question or
> is struggling and needs encouragement. I may also give one to
> the group to ask them to rethink something that they may have
> ignored or to revisit an earlier decision that took them down the
> wrong path.

To the outsider, the experienced facilitator (working in a classroom of
experienced kids) makes all this look easy. There's no long line of students
waiting with questions and no one off-task; industriousness and creativity
rule the day. For the beginner, however, this first moment can look chaotic.
It can be unnerving to see students struggle, to look helplessly at you
for guidance.

When students struggle, state and restate clearly what you expect to
see and hear while the students are working so that they know what is
expected and can effectively take action. Step aside and observe carefully

as the students work. Refrain from rescuing groups that seem to be in trouble; let them struggle with the task they have undertaken. How long should a group struggle? That depends on a lot of things, but usually you can let them struggle longer than you think you can. Ask questions if necessary in order to refocus a group:

- What are you supposed to be working on?
- What steps have you already taken?
- What isn't working?
- What do you need to be successful? Where can you get it?
- What else could you be doing?

Al's advice to the beginning facilitator is to plan in advance:

As a novice teacher, I wrote down a script of the things I needed to work on and look for. I gave myself a couple of questions I could always use like "What do you think?" I even put up a couple of posters on the back wall that said things like "Wait time," because I knew that I tended to answer my own questions. I fine-tuned these and changed them over time with each class.

Sometimes the wheels come off, particularly when you and your students are just getting used to this new way of learning together. Perhaps you look around the room and realize that most students aren't working, or they are working but not on what they should be doing. Maybe participation is uneven, with some students hard at work and others loafing. Maybe you see much effort directed in the wrong direction—four students working on a beautiful visual aid filled with incorrect information or a spirited discussion over an insignificant point of content. These are the moments when inexperienced Next Gen instructors throw up their hands and say, "See? I told you this wouldn't work. My kids just can't handle this kind of responsibility." They're wrong, however. At this moment, the wise educator recognizes that it's time to step in, not to tell students what they should be doing but to ask the right questions to remind them of what they need to do, and why. (Don't undervalue the "why." Many kids can't do work like this until they understand and internalize the "why.")

In Erin Hunter's carpentry classroom, her first response when things aren't working is often a straightforward "What the heck are you people doing?" Then she utilizes carefully selected coaching questions to ferret out the specific problem or issue preventing success.

It could be as simple as, "Did you feel like you understood what the goal was?" I ask myself, was it me—the way I posed the problem? Is it group dynamics? Is it a grouping issue—does everyone not have something to do? It's a very responsive thing based on what I perceive, what my gut tells me is going on. That being said, I often fall back on six basic prompts when debriefing failure or less-than-successful results:

1. What I learned was . . .

2. What I found interesting about this work was . . .

3. What surprised me was . . .

4. I want to know more about . . .

5. Right now I'm feeling . . .

6. This experience might have been more valuable to me if . . .

We start there. Then it's all based on what they said they were aiming for. Same with content: If it seems like they're not getting the content I want them to get, then it's about using focused coaching questions to get them redirected toward what they don't know, what they're not doing, so we can make a plan to get back on track.

Al adds,

> 66 If the teacher admits mistakes openly, then kids can feel safe in taking risks (and potentially making mistakes) too.
> —Al Magnusson   99

You can throw it back to them. Ask them to circle it up and discuss: "What's going on? What do we need to do?" You can put up a T-chart with those questions. Sometimes it's that we don't have the resources they need, they don't understand a concept and I need to reteach it, or the goal is too hard. Sometimes I have to say, "That's not quite the right thing. Let's change that part—it's too much or it's too easy—and let's do something different."

Then I apologize—always apologize when you mess up. Some teachers are scared to say "I was wrong." But you have to be able to say, "Let's back up, make adjustments, and start again." That's hard for novice teachers to admit, but it's okay. It's completely okay. In fact, it's necessary. If the teacher admits mistakes openly, then kids can feel safe in taking risks (and potentially making mistakes) too. When you ask the kids to help you figure out how to adjust so you better meet their needs, that's when you become part of the collaboration. That's a giant step forward.

Jenn takes a similar tack.

I guide students by asking several questions. I ask questions to help the students clarify what they are trying to do and what they have done that is not working. It is important to know where the students are going wrong to help them find their way back.

You can't always just give them the same directions over and over again. If a friend calls you saying that they got lost on the way to your house, you first need to know where they are before you can tell them where to go. It's also important to know how they got to where they are, so they don't make the same mistake in the future. If you just give the same directions again but your friend is lost and on a different road, your directions are not going to be helpful. You may have made a mistake in your directions, or maybe your friend needed more landmarks to look for or mileage to watch for on the odometer. No matter what, the goal was to get your friend to your house, and you need to give them what they need to get there, even if it means you drive to them and let them follow you to your house. The same is true for teaching. If the students do not understand you, you need to evaluate what you are doing and what each individual student needs to help meet the goal. You may need to provide more guided practice or more explicit directions than what you anticipated, and that's okay.

For Louise,

It is seldom an entire group; it is usually just individuals. It is important to let that individual know, privately, rather than upend the entire class. (When the entire group goes astray, it is seldom a hands-on situation but rather a sit-and-listen lesson.) If a workday seems off and less productive, I will have them take a moment and rate themselves from 1 to 5 against the expectations for the day. I will then go around and say I agree or saw more or less. This way they know I am watching, and the next day tends to go more smoothly.

As always, the issue is often one of clarity of expectations.

Trust your gut. If you do not like the way the class is operating, call a time-out and process what you're seeing. If a trend is developing (too much nonproductive noise, students being off-task or just sitting while others work, etc.), point it out to the class and brainstorm options to resolve the situation. Use this new problem as an opportunity for new learning. It will be tempting to "save" your students, to provide them with more information about what they should do and exactly how they should do it. It is

> 66 It will be tempting to 'save' your students, to provide them with more information about what they should do and exactly how they should do it. It is imperative that you resist this impulse. 99

imperative that you resist this impulse. When we "do for" our students, we steal the learning experience.

Classroom facilitators most often fail because they expect too much too soon. You're asking your students to do something completely new. (Heck, you're asking yourself to do something completely new as well—be gentle with yourself as you're learning.) They'll need you to support them by planning carefully—and then by getting out of their way. In Erin's words, this may look like this:

> Me, standing there, drinking coffee, watching and listening. I might be specifically listening for levels of conversation: Are they talking to each other about the challenge? Are they just running off and working individually because they don't know they're sup-posed to work together? Have they organized themselves? Are they just trying to look busy because they think they're supposed to? I'm listening for any indication of confusion, of being pointed down the wrong track, so that, if necessary, I can redirect them.

For the Next Generation instructor, that redirection comes in the form of questions:

- What are you working on? Why?
- What are you hoping to gain by going in this direction?
- What does the assignment ask you to do? How do you know?

Erin may guide them further by asking specific questions: "What's the difference between a hand tool and a power tool? Have you ever used a power tool? What are some of the power tools you've used?" The right question at the right time can be enough to refocus the group's efforts, allowing Erin to slip back out of the group—the most important part of coaching. In the Gaming phase, the teacher's most important job is to remain quiet, particularly when it's difficult to do so.

The Gaming phase of the process requires the teacher to have a specific skill set. It requires conscientious observation and a willingness to watch and wait. It also requires the instructor to be fully present in the classroom, even when he or she is not central to the work being done. It can be tempting to take care of paperwork, to send one more e-mail, to deal with the mountain of tasks to be done every day. However, being fully present when making observations, seeing what is really happening, will allow you to gain new insights into what your students know and can do. It will enable you to understand what they're thinking, and it will help you to ask better questions. It's easier to be fully present when you have clarity about what you're looking for, but keep an open mind about student activity you may not have expected.

Anna Kay Vorsteg, executive director of the American Youth Founda-tion, provided my first formal training in facilitation. One key point has always stayed with me: "Eat a Bit-O-Honey." For the uninitiated, the Bit-O-Honey is a toffee/candy concoction whose key attribute is unyielding stickiness. To eat a Bit-O-Honey is to commit oneself to at least five minutes of lockjaw. Speech is impossible. For a beginning facilitator, the Bit-O-Honey is the key to success because the impulse to provide more instruction, to correct early mistakes, and to solve problems for students is almost irresistible. The Bit-O-Honey will keep you quiet long enough to observe the first moves your students make with a very visceral, very sweet reminder that they are the ones doing this work, not you.

In those first moments—and many moments after—your students will ask questions. Most of these will be questions that they already know how to answer. Learned helplessness is endemic in our schools. Don't be afraid to turn students' questions back to them, using almost the same language. If they ask, "Where are the scissors?" it's fine to respond with the same question, asked with sincerity and without even a hint of sarcasm. They'll figure it out if the information and resources have been provided beforehand. Many teachers use the "ask three and then me" approach noted by Dan earlier, requiring students to ask three peers before approaching a teacher with a question. Others make Question Asker an assigned role within the group. Allowing students to answer their own questions is easy when you know the answer or the question is very concrete (the scissors are on the table by the door) but harder when the question is more abstract ("What are we supposed to do again?") or you don't know the answer ("What should we do? The computer is down, and we can't get our presentation to load.").

Also, the impulse to provide an answer never completely goes away. The wise educator recognizes that answering the questions for oneself is what learning is all about. If we answer all the questions, what are the students doing?

BOX 4.3   MY FAVORITE QUESTIONS FOR RESPONDING TO (STUDENT) QUESTIONS

- "Hmm . . . I don't know. Where *are* the _____?"
- "What does your group think about that?"
- "Who might know the answer to that question?"
- "That sounds tricky. How could you solve that?"
- "What else could you do?"
- "What does it say on the assignment sheet?
- "What's your role/job/goal again?"
- "What could you do differently to make that work better for you?"
- "You're right—that is hard. I look forward to seeing how you figure that out."
- "That's a problem—you're right. But it's not my problem; it's yours. What do you need to do to solve it?"

The National School Reform Initiative calls the above questions "probing questions" and offers the following suggestions as well (some of these were drawn from Charlotte Danielson's *Pathwise* work):

- Why do you think this is the case?
- What would have to change in order for...?
- What do you feel is right in your heart?
- What do you wish...?
- What's another way you might...?
- What would it look like if...?
- How was...different from...?
- What sort of an impact do you think...?
- What criteria did you use to...?
- When have you done/experienced something like this before?
- What might you see happening in your group if...?
- How did you decide/determine/conclude...?
- What is your hunch about...?
- What was your intention when...?
- What do you assume to be true about...?
- What is the connection between...and...?
- What if the opposite were true? Then what?
- How might your assumptions about...have influenced how you are thinking about...?
- Why is this such a dilemma for you?

Source: Adapted from Thompson-Grove, Frazer, & Dunne, 2006. Adapted with permission.

Obviously, as with all elements of facilitation, we walk a fine line between challenging and overwhelming. Students need to see and hear us acknowledge that this is hard work and, at the same time, that we have absolute and total faith that they can—and will—do what we expect of them.

So what if they fail? What if the task was too advanced, if they lacked the skills or the wherewithal to achieve the goal, if they ran out of time, or if they just didn't get it? What then? This is the beauty of facilitation: It provides a platform from which you can make true the old saying "We learn more from failure than success." By processing the experience, surfacing what went wrong and what went right, what students understand and what they still don't get, you can target the next activity very carefully toward their success. You'll also have made clear to your students that you're serious about this new way of learning and that you'll let them reap

❝ You'll also have made clear to your students that you're serious about this new way of learning and that you'll let them reap the negative consequences of their classroom choices—but that you'll help them get up when they fall. ❞

the negative consequences of their classroom choices—but that you'll help them get up when they fall.

In one of my 10th-grade English classes, I tasked students with the challenge of staging a scene from *Romeo and Juliet*. Each group was to select and stage a different scene, making (possibly nontraditional) choices about the best ways to convey that scene's meaning to the rest of the class. We worked for two weeks, and the scenes were just awful. The students had all chosen traditional staging and had focused on memorizing the words instead of conveying the meaning. What I'd hoped for were interesting, funny, over-staged, overacted scenes that clearly conveyed what the students thought about who the characters were, what they were thinking and feeling, and what the scene was about. This obviously hadn't been clear to the students, and they'd delivered what they thought I wanted—lines of rote, regurgitated verse. In debriefing the experience, I asked the students to talk about what they understood about the characters and the play now that they hadn't understood before. They had nothing. They didn't understand anything new; they'd just memorized because they thought they were supposed to. I was horrified.

I reframed the assignment, not by modeling what I wanted, but by asking them to create scenes that clearly communicated the characters' intentions and desires using modern language, costumes, and staging. I gave them one period (and two nights at home) to prepare, and I checked in constantly, asking if they understood what they were supposed to do. Could they tell me what was expected of them, using their own words? What was their plan? Their vision? What did they think the characters wanted? What did they think the scene was about? The final performances met—and exceeded—my expectations.

It's not enough for me to know what students have learned, however. They must also have a chance to own their learning, to assess what they've gained and what they still need to know, and to celebrate their hard work. The next chapter will guide you through this process, also known as the Claiming and Exclaiming stages.

5

Claiming and Exclaiming

Reflection

In a world without resources, we always have the kids. They're free. And they are always experts on what is going on inside their heads.

—Rob Fried

Reflection (aka Claiming) is the final piece of the facilitation puzzle. When we reflect, we make meaning of what we've experienced, we connect new information to existing knowledge and desires—in short, we learn. Without the opportunity to reflect, we may temporarily memorize information, we may even memorize it permanently in a Trivial Pursuit sort of way, but we don't really learn. Reflective time and techniques, however, are nearly unheard of in classrooms today.

CLAIMING

Aptly named, Claiming (also known as reflection) is the process by which your students lay claim to their own learning. It can happen at the end of

Figure 5.1   Framework for Next Generation Instruction: Claiming

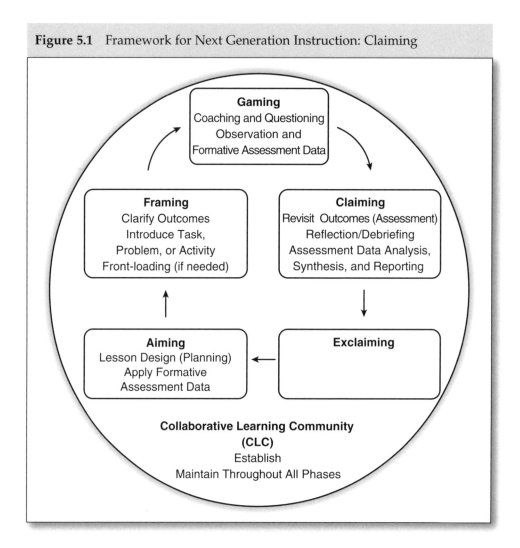

the lesson or class and at the culmination of larger projects and experiences or any combination of those times. Next Generation instructors gain information about their students' understanding of what they know and can do—their metacognitive growth—during this stage. Claiming is where we help students process their experiences and transfer new content and process knowledge to their next task.

Traditional assessment, if you choose to use those methods, can happen as a lead-in to this stage. Students can reflect on what they thought they knew and whether that learning was reflected on the exam or the quiz. If pretests were used, comparing pretests to postassessments could measure growth and provide fodder for interesting conversation. Jenn Huard notes,

> It is essential to debrief learning and new discoveries with students. Some students make connections with little discussion or coaching, while others need to hear several other students' connections. I think students tend to do best when they can debrief learning in a conversation. Sometimes, having students write reflections and then sharing them out the day after in a whole group is more useful. Making connections can help students connect more deeply with material and enable them to transfer knowledge from one concept to another.

This is another place where technology, used well, can be an asset. Students can use video diaries or group blogs to document their processes and their reflections on the results.

In Al Magnusson's classroom, claiming connects back to framing:

> I created something I call a new SPIN on learning. SPIN is an acronym: S = Superior, P = Proficient, I = Intermediate, and N = Novice. At the beginning of the unit, I give students the curriculum in "I Can" statements—for example, "I Can graph speed data,"—and ask them to assess themselves using SPIN. The first couple of times, I'll walk them through it to be sure they're thinking about what they know and don't know. I'll be careful and descriptive in my explanation, and they write down what they think they know and how well they know it. Then we do it again, maybe in the middle of the unit or at the end of the unit, and they discover that they know more, that they've moved up a bit. Over the course of the unit, they gain confidence because they feel like they're connected to the curriculum. They look ahead and become invested in what we're doing.
>
> Now, this doesn't count as part of their grade per se, and I find that kids need help sometimes. I'll look down and say, "You still think you're a novice at that? Why? Don't you know how to do x, y, and z? I think you're a bit higher than that." Or, especially at the beginning, I'll see some wise guy giving all Ss, so I'll say, "Are you really? 'Cause all Ss gets you an oral exam right here, right now." It's a great way for them to really get an idea of what they know and don't know.

Examples of SPIN rubrics can be found in Figures 5.2–5.4.

Figure 5.2 Physical Science (Classical Mechanics) Learning Level Data Table

(S = Superior, P = Proficient, I = Intermediate, N = Novice)

Big Question: How do matter and energy interact?

Name _____ Class _____

I can . . .	Date	Date	Date	Date	Date	Date	Date
I can accurately **measure** and **calculate** for speed and velocity.							
I can accurately **graph** speed data.							
I can **organize** through an engineering project from brainstorming to blueprinting to parts design to construction to a creative paint job to a final motion capability.							
I can **demonstrate** the use of a variety of science tools to develop and implement a major design-engineering project.							
I can **examine** the differences between potential and kinetic energy and provide real-life applications of them.							
I can **demonstrate** the effect of motion (position, direction, speed, balanced/unbalanced force) on an object.							
I can **construct** a working model that demonstrates energy transformation and conservation of energy. *							
I can **observe** and **describe** the force of gravity and its effects.							
I can **interpret** various formulas (work, speed, etc.). (include mechanical advantages of simple machines)							
I can accurately **review** data that allow for a hypothesis about the effect of multiple forces on an object in motion. (Ts. design whole-class data table)							
I can **examine** objects with new technology and **determine** design features that show their use and function. (Ts. use gadgets, old stuff, etc.)							
I can **analyze** the basic principles of Newton's three laws of motion.							

Source: Al Magnusson. Used with permission.

Figure 5.3 Chemistry Learning Level Data Table

(S = Superior, P = Proficient, I = Intermediate, N = Novice)

Name _____

Central Question: How do matter and energy interact at the atomic level?

I can . . .	Date	Date	Date	Date	Date	Date	Date	Date
. . . **differentiate among** atoms, elements, molecules, and compounds.								
. . . **identify** characteristics of mixtures.								
. . . **explain** conservation of matter (w/ data, total mass stays the same, even if substances interact)								
. . . **interpret** chemical equations.								
. . . **illustrate** the relationship of weight, mass, volume, and density.								
. . . **compare** and **contrast** substances when given specific data.(melting, boiling, density, solubility)								
. . . **illustrate** the states of matter. (energy, molecular action, temperature)								
. . . **explain** how substances change chemically with other substances. (form new substances [compounds], change properties, oxidize (burn/rust), reaction factors)								
. . . **trace** a real-world energy transformation via a chemical and/or heat system.								
. . . **distinguish** heat transfer through radiation, conduction, and convection.								
. . . **discuss** the advancement of chemistry and how scientific technology can help identify, understand, and potentially solve local and global issues. (alternative energy, current energy resources, durable/nondurable goods)								
. . . **describe** various scientific tools and use them to measure and calculate. (students can list here)								

Figure 5.4 Biology Learning Level Data Table

(S = Superior, P = Proficient, I = Intermediate, N = Novice)

Name _____

Central Question: How do matter and energy interact with living beings?

I can . . .	Date	Date	Date	Date	Date	Date	Date	Date
. . . **identify** living vs. nonliving and **account for** the classification of living beings.								
. . . **compare** and **contrast** the structures and processes of animal and plant cells.								
. . . **compare** and **contrast** respiration and photosynthesis.								
. . . show the **significance** of how different organisms have coordinated systems to maintain life. (get energy, grow, move, respond, defend, reproduce, maintain homeostasis)								
. . . **differentiate between** asexual and sexual reproduction.								
. . . **identify** the role of certain human body systems and **describe** their interactions. (and **compare** w/ other vertebrates)								
. . . **illustrate** the organization of cells, tissues, organs, and systems. (w/ internal regulation) *								
. . . **trace** the process of fertilization.								
. . . **distinguish** the three stages of human embryonic development.								
. . . using data, **analyze** genetic information. (DNA, chromosomes and traits)								
. . . **summarize** how diseases can affect humans via intrinsic failures or infection. (viruses, bacteria, fungi, parasites/abiotic and biotic/white blood cells)								
. . . **review** how technology has influenced the growth of scientific knowledge in biology. (local and global issues, medical improvements, medical waste, biotechnology, careers, *water cleaning*)								

Reflection—also known as Claiming—is based in three simple concepts:

1. **Concrete recall.** What did I do?

2. **Evaluation.** How effective were my efforts?

3. **Transfer.** What would I do differently if I were starting over now (or next time)?

There are myriad rephrasings of these questions, each carefully designed to fit a particular need, project, or class. Table 5.5 offers alternatives for each level of question.

Figure 5.5   Questions to Prompt Claiming (Reflection)

Concrete Recall	Evaluation	Transfer
What happened to you?	What difference did you make?	What caused that to happen?
What was the group supposed to do—what was the task assigned? Who did what first?	Did you complete the task?	What have you learned related to the academic areas you are studying?
Then what happened?	Did you do it adequately, poorly, or very well? Why?	How would it have been different if X had occurred?
What specific steps did you take?	Were you successful?	What does this experience mean for you? For the community?
In what order did you do them?	Did you get the results you hoped for?	What lessons can you take from this to apply next time?
What did you observe?	Did you learn a new skill?	How could that skill be useful in the future?
What did you see or hear that surprised you?	How was your experience different from what you expected?	What seem to be the root causes of that?
Who talked? Who didn't talk?	What did you like/dislike about this activity?	What should we be sure to do next time? Why?
Whose ideas were used? Whose ideas weren't used?	What did you learn about the people in our class?	What will you (could you) do with that new knowledge?
What roles did different people play?	How were people helped and/or helpful?	What would you like to see happen again? Not happen again?

Sources: Cairn & Coble, 1993 (adapted with permission from "Learning by Giving: K–8 Service-Learning Curriculum Guide" © 1993 by National Youth Leadership Council, www.nylc.org); Frank, 2004; University of Minnesota, Community Service-Learning Center, 2011.

Reflection, the process of dissecting an experience in order to glean long-term learning from a single experience or a set of experiences, is an oft-overlooked tool in the teachers' arsenal. When we reflect, we make meaning of what we've experienced, and we connect new information and skills to existing knowledge and desires—in short, we learn. Without the opportunity to reflect, we may temporarily memorize information, or we may even memorize it permanently in a Trivial Pursuit sort of way, but we don't really learn how to use what we know when we need to. We don't gain the capacity to apply our knowledge to different settings and situations. In short, we don't grow.

> ❝ Reflection is a *bridge* connecting one experience to another; a *comma*, providing a pause in which to think and question; and a *mirror* in which to view personal and group behaviors. It is the linchpin in the learning process. ❞

Reflection is a *bridge* connecting one experience to another; a *comma*, providing a pause in which to think and question; and a *mirror* in which to view personal and group behaviors. It is the linchpin in the learning process. Accordingly, it is imperative that reflective practices become second nature in selecting and facilitating activities for and with students. Reflective questioning is the process of looking at experience through three simple, elegant lenses. First, we review the *concrete sequence of events* and actions that were taken in order to clarify a common experience upon which all can agree. It's not uncommon for three members of the same group to have vastly different recall of who did what and when they did it, even during a very short activity.

Second, after the concrete has been agreed upon, the group must *evaluate the effectiveness* of those steps in meeting the challenge given to them. If, for example, the task was to find examples of amphibians, their habitats, and their primary food sources, then the group's action of visiting the library might have been a very good choice. If most group members were unfamiliar with how to locate resources in the library, however, it might have been a poor choice. The group is simply evaluating the effectiveness of the steps taken in helping the group to complete the task given.

The final element of the reflective process asks students to *transfer their learning*—to apply their current experience to future situations, real or imaginary. Students might have the chance to go back and redo a portion of the project, thereby making the question "What would you do differently if you could start over?" very appropriate. In other cases, students benefit from supposing the way that their work processes or products might have been different had one variable been changed. For example, how would the group have worked together differently had it been smaller? Larger? What if students had done this project alone? What if they'd broken the project down into smaller steps?

Some students benefit from the use of creative fiction as a tool for transfer. Writing a story or creating a skit or video about what they wish they had done in their process or how they could use their new skills in the future can be very helpful. Other students appreciate a more practical, realistic process. If the class had researched the ins and outs of voter registration and created promotional materials for a local voter registration drive, then the conversation around "What if voting were unsafe in our country? What if it were illegal?" could be not only intriguing but also an excellent way to connect students' personal experience to the larger curriculum (Cairn & Coble, 1993). Such metacognitive transfer is result of quality reflection.

For the Otter Valley team, reflection is about regrouping and conversation, based on reflective questions and written responses, and through formal and/or informal debriefing, based on rubrics and written feedback from teachers and peers. According to the team, metacognitive transfer is rooted in the reality that

> projects build on one another throughout the year. Earlier projects have more scaffolding; later ones are messier. Since we have all seen ninth graders struggle with the traditional English and social studies research papers, we fill our year with research projects and offer lots of support. We don't try to teach the whole process at once. Early projects include a few steps/skills required in research writing. Finally, by the last project, students have been through all the steps several times, have received feedback, and have used the applicable rubrics. They know what to expect and for the most part can do it on their own.

Individual reflection is an internal process. Teachers need an external representation of that process, however, in order to understand the student's progress. The most accurate representation is going to be one that matches the way the student thinks—the student's learning style. Reflection tools might include the following. (More detailed instructions for items marked * can be found in Chapter 6.)

- Speaking in small or large groups
- Teaching material to other students
- Planning future projects
- Role-playing
- Creating photo essays or video presentations
- Keeping a sketchbook
- Writing poetry or fiction
- Diagramming processes
- Performing skits
- "Rating" activities (e.g., Fist to Five*, thumbs-up/down)

- Postcards or Found Objects*
- Body Parts*
- Sculpture
- Collage
- Blogs/wikis
- Timelines
- Think/Pair/Share *
- Video diaries
- Personal essays
- PowerPoint presentations (Frank, 2003)

This is one of the times that you *most* want to play to a student's strengths, particularly when the reflection is part of a summative assessment or if it occurs at a major transition point in the course (end of unit, completion of large presentations or projects, etc.). Briefer techniques (exit slips, Fist to Five*, End-of-Day Sheets*, using thumbs-up/middle/down, etc.) are sufficient for quick, formative assessments of student understanding or progress. Teachers must move beyond the traditional "journaling as primary tool for reflection" paradigm. Learning logs with specific prompts (as opposed to journals, which are often overly personal and wide ranging in their content), End-of-Day Sheets*, group blogs, "tweets" (utilizing Twitter or just asking students to write their responses in 140 characters or less), and exit slips can all provide a written means of reflection, but reflection need not take written form. The questions are the spine of the reflective experience, but the medium can be as varied as the imagination. Students can reflect via large- or small-group discussions, presentations, drawings, scrapbooks, photo essays, or PowerPoint. The important aspect is the examination of the experience through the three lenses: concrete, evaluation, and transfer.

Al Magnusson has a small number of reflective components in his toolbox, but he uses them quite often.

> For me, using a lot of different tools means it will take time for the kids to learn how to complete them thoroughly, and this time is better spent reflecting than learning a bunch of new reflection tools. When the students work collaboratively, I have them discuss what went well with the group process. Then I have them reflect individually on this process, and here I have them talk about what improvements might have helped the group to work better together. They also reflect on the product that was generated. Then the students explore how their individual input contributed to the process. I even go further as I ask them to judge how much they think they learned with this learning objective.
>
> I have also developed some simple forms that have students reflect on the skill progress. Targeted skills are self-direction,

collaboration, organization, and leadership. Reflecting on these every week or so—using these forms and class discussion—allows the culture of the classroom to develop a common language toward understanding what progress students can make with these life skills.

I also have frequent academic checks at the end of classes. A simple "exit slip" asks students to answer three to five questions on the content. This helps me track students individually with their science understanding. (Please realize that if I have any students who are significantly challenged with written words, then they can draw or speak their thoughts to me when necessary.) Also, a well-placed, straightforward "How do you think things are going right now?" or "How was class today?" goes a long way toward realigning the students with their work, be it group or even individual assignments. This classroom culture hopefully helps kids to recognize the power and value of reflection as part of their lifelong learning.

Another tool I use is a reflective midterm progress report and end-of-quarter "report card," which the students use and then share with their parents and then give back to me . . . something I call the "communication loop." Parents love this . . . and I do too. . . . The comments back from the parents are very rewarding and affirming of this classroom culture I have established.

Jenn uses a similar set of tools:

To transfer meta-knowledge from one lesson to the next or even one class to the next, coaching students with well-crafted questions will help them make connections. Doing chalk talks, KWLs (Know/Want to Know/Need to Learn or Have Learned), and having discussions are other ways to transfer knowledge.

When reflection is built into part of the typical day, when students become used to being asked for their evaluation of their work and their processes, when classroom practice is modified based on student feedback ("We need another day in the library," or "We don't know how to use PowerPoint well enough to make this presentation any good."), then students begin to believe that they aren't passive recipients of information or mute passengers on the educational

> 66 Reflection can be a short conversation at the end of a class period. . . . It can be a longer conversation at the end of a project, during which students talk about their processes and make notes about what they want to do differently next time—notes that they refer to again at the *beginning* of the next project. 99

bus. The time taken for reflection doesn't have to be great, but it must be intentional. Students must have the chance to reflect at transitional moments in the day. They must be guided in looking back at earlier efforts and forward in preparation for their next steps. Reflection can be as simple as a brief conversation around appropriate behavior before an assembly. It can be a short conversation at the end of a class period in which students review the goals for the day and assess how they did individually and as a class, potentially even setting goals for the following day. It can be a longer conversation at the end of a project, during which students talk about their processes and make notes about what they want to do differently next time—notes that they refer to again at the *beginning* of the next project. In my public-speaking classroom, this often took the form of a self-evaluation due at the end of the class period in which the student spoke. The student was required to reflect on the speech and on the previous self-evaluation, answering the following questions:

1. What was my goal for this speech?

2. What did I do to make steps towards that goal?

3. Did I achieve the goal? How do I know?

4. What is my goal for my next speech?

Students were required to hand in their self-evaluations as "exit" slips. The grade for the speech didn't get recorded unless the self-evaluation was turned in. (They were also required to provide feedback to the two speakers immediately following their own presentation. The peer feedback they received provided fodder for their own self-assessments.) We referred to those goals at the beginning of every class period and again at the end of every class period. Students knew that, during the first five minutes of class, they were to locate their last self-evaluation and check in on their goals for the upcoming speech. They knew I expected them to have a specific plan for meeting those goals and that I would check—not every day and not on everyone—but I would check. And they knew that the last five minutes of class would be given over to a quick reflective piece that would require them to evaluate their work. We also planned for spontaneous reflection, examining processes and work as they emerged. All that reflection counted for a grade—we even had a reflection rubric. It was a big part of their grade, but, more important, it was a big part of our learning community.

Reflections can be documented on notebook paper, a handout, chart pack, or overheads and through student response systems, Poll Everywhere, texts, e-mails, Twitter, or an interactive whiteboard template. Use the tools you have available and use them often.

By integrating past learning into future situations (both academic and social), we can help our students become that ubiquitous feature of mission statements everywhere: the Lifelong Learner. In order to facilitate that transfer, however, we must help students first to identify previously gained skills (finding a book in the library, locating a place on a map, determining the volume of a polyhedron, etc.) and then to apply them to new tasks or challenges. By repeatedly and transparently moving students through the process of reflection and transfer, we can help students generalize the common underlying principles received from previous experiences (e.g., problem solving, self-management, listening, asking questions, offering a different perspective respectfully).

In Erin Hunter's classroom, reflection occurs on both the community and individual levels with both pre- and postlesson reflections, which support the transfer of learning from one activity to the next.

> If, in a prior [lesson], they created a T chart to reflect on how well they did and what they wanted to improve, then [before the next lesson] they'd look at it and say, "What do we want to work on this time?" Then they'd pick one thing—collaboration, making sure everyone had job to do, something like that.

Students then define the attributes of that targeted skill—what it will look like and sound like when done well, perhaps, or what they want Erin to be looking for as they work. This new list of attributes then becomes the rubric for assessing their performance during the lesson or unit.

> For example, let's say they said, "We're not making sure everyone has something to do." Then we target that skill (collaboration) on the next challenge. Then at the end of the challenge, I remind them, "You said you wanted to work on making sure everyone had a valuable something to do—to feel a part of the process. How did that go for you? What went well? What didn't? What do you want to do differently next time?" And that just sets the stage for the next thing we do.

Erin uses a combination of paper-and-pencil tools using common, repeated prompts and more active techniques.

> I've written several [lessons] that specifically target reflection. In one, they had to come up with a skit that represented what they had learned that semester. (They were a very creative, very physical class, so they loved to get up and act out what they'd done.) Another task was to create a puzzle that represented all the pieces of knowledge— both content and process—they'd learned and how it fit together.

Allison uses a technique she calls the Autopsy, in which the students dissect the process and the product, combined with entrance and exit slips focusing on specific learning.

> I use it as a way to get students to think about the quality of their work, what they might do better the next time, what they are proud of. I want to see what they've learned and to get them to see what they learned, and I use that as feedback for me about how to frame other work or how to reframe this process for the next time.

Jenn's reflection work is based in schoolwide expectations for learning.

> Students often reflect on their performance, growth, and experiences in relation to the Souhegan Six or Mission Statement (see Box 5.1). It is important for students to make connections and reflect so they have a better opportunity to remember what they learned and to learn from their mistakes. Similarly, as an educator, I reflect often on my daily practice. I also elicit feedback from students and parents to find areas where I should improve my practice. Other teachers are always there to listen and help problem-solve and offer a different perspective.

BOX 5.1

Souhegan High School Mission Statement

Souhegan High School aspires to be a community of learners born of respect, trust, and courage.
We consciously commit ourselves

- to support and engage an individual's unique gifts, passions, and intentions.
- to develop and empower the mind, body, and heart.
- to challenge and expand the comfortable limits of thought, tolerance, and performance.
- to inspire and honor the active stewardship of family, nation, and globe.

Souhegan Six–Souhegan High School Behavioral Expectations

1. Respect and encourage the right to teach and the right to learn at all times.
2. Be actively engaged in the learning; ask questions, collaborate, and seek solutions.
3. Be on time to fulfill your daily commitments.
4. Be appropriate; demonstrate behavior that is considerate of the community, the campus, and yourself.
5. Be truthful; communicate honestly.
6. Be responsible and accountable for your choices.

Used with permission.

You may find that you need to be able to give students credit for their reflection in the form of a letter grade, a check mark, or a point total. All the more need for a rubric describing quality reflection or, at the very least, a clearly posted set of quality criteria that you review before setting students to the task of reflection.

Kim Carter and the QED Foundation have provided us with an excellent example of a reflection rubric (Figure 5.6), which you may choose to use as is or change to meet your own needs. In any case, it will provide a starting point as you and your students develop something that will allow you not only to assign an authentic grade but also to guide students toward authentic, powerful reflection. Less complex but equally useful examples can be found in Figures 5.7–5.9.

Reflection allows students the opportunity to think about, make meaning from, and analyze their experiences to "get the learning out" of these experiences. Through reflection, students develop and adjust their short- and long-term goals, explore problems and solutions encountered during their learning, and connect their experiences to their learning goals.

Reflection is an important part of the feedback loop between the student and certified school personnel and, if applicable, mentor. Therefore, sharing the learning with certified school personnel and mentors in a timely manner allows the student to receive formative guidance through timely responses to the reflection, increasing his or her learning.

Figure 5.6   Reflection Rubric

	Beginning	Progressing	Proficient	Exemplary
Trait 1: How does the student use **goal setting** to manage his/her learning?	The student identifies short- or long-term goals.	The student identifies short- and/or long-term goals and uses them to determine tasks and next steps.	The student identifies short- and long-term goals, adjusts them as necessary, and determines tasks and next steps in achieving his/her goals.	The student identifies, evaluates, and revises his/her short-term goals as needed and is able to justify changes made along the way, explaining how this leads to successfully meeting his/her long-term goals.
Trait 2: How does the student connect his/her experiences with **targeted** competencies?	The student communicates about experiences; however, connections to	The student communicates about experiences and makes a connection to	The student communicates about and analyzes the connections between	The student communicates about and analyzes the connections between experiences and targeted

(Continued)

Figure 5.6 (Continued)

	Beginning	Progressing	Proficient	Exemplary
	targeted competencies are not made.	targeted competencies.	specific experiences and targeted competencies.	competencies and predicts future behaviors/decisions based on his/her analysis ("Next time . . .").
Trait 3: How does the student deal with **challenges/ problems** encountered during his/her learning experience?	The student identifies problem(s).	The student describes problem(s) and states possible solution(s).	The student describes and analyzes problem(s), states solutions, and assesses solutions for the problem(s).	The student describes and analyzes problems, assesses solutions for the problems, identifies a chosen solution for a specific problem, and evaluates the effectiveness of his/her choice.
Trait 4: How does the **student's thinking** develop as a result of his/her learning experience?	The student summarizes personal experiences.	The student makes connections between a personal idea and an experience to establish the basis of a reflection.	The student analyzes his/her own growth by making connections between personal ideas and his/her learning experiences.	The student analyzes his/her own growth by making connections between personal ideas and his/her learning experiences, leading the student to new perspectives or insights.
Trait 5: How does the student use appropriate language, vocabulary, syntax, and grammar to **communicate effectively** with his/her mentor and certified school personnel?	The student demonstrates a lack of control over media-appropriate language, including vocabulary, syntax, and grammar. Reflection is not in an organized structure. Errors disrupt the flow of communication.	The student demonstrates inconsistent control of media-appropriate language, including vocabulary, syntax, and grammar. Organization of the reflection's structure may or may not be evident. Errors detract from communication.	The student demonstrates control of media-appropriate language, including vocabulary, syntax, and grammar, within an organized structure. Errors do not interfere with communication.	The student demonstrates control of media-appropriate language, including vocabulary, syntax, and grammar, within an organized structure. Few if any errors. Intention of thought is clearly communicated.

Source: Carter & QED Assessment Moderation Team, 2011. Used with permission.

Figure 5.7   Reflection Rubric

Student: _____   Date:_____

Criteria	Response to Content	Personal Thoughts and Feelings	Examples
1	Student does not state an opinion in the reflection.	Student does not state an opinion in the reflection.	Student includes no examples in the reflection.
2	Student briefly states opinion in the reflection.	Student includes few thoughts and feelings in the reflection.	Student includes few examples in the reflection.
3	Student briefly states an opinion in the reflection.	Student includes some thoughts and feelings in the reflection.	Student includes examples in the reflection.
4	Student gives an in-depth explanation of his/her opinion in the reflection.	Student includes many thoughts and feelings in the reflection.	Student includes many examples in the reflection.
Total			

Teacher Comments:

Figure 5.8   Reflection Rubric

Name:_____   Date:_____

4

All questions are answered in complete sentences that restate the question.

All answers are factually correct.

All answers are explained clearly.

3

All questions are answered in complete sentences, but not all restate the question.

There are some minor factual mistakes.

All answers are explained.

2

All questions are answered, but the answers are not all in complete sentences.

There are factual mistakes.

Some, but not all, answers are explained.

(Continued)

Figure 5.8 (Continued)

> **1**
> Not all questions are answered.
> There are major factual mistakes.
> Most answers are not explained.

Figure 5.9   Reflection Rubric

Name: _____

Period: _____   Date: _____

Does your reflection include:

- ☐ Name?
- ☐ Date?
- ☐ Prompt?
- ☐ Description of what you did?
- ☐ Evaluation of how it worked?
- ☐ Analysis of why it worked (or didn't)?
- ☐ Plans for what you'll do next time?

Comments:

EXCLAIMING

After you've completed Claiming (reflection), allow a time and place for Exclaiming (celebration), the acknowledgment of the positive aspects of students' experiences, including those that were uncomfortable. Your celebration choices can be important rituals and elements in maintaining your collaborative learning community. Something as small as a class cheer; a round of applause; a two-minute "dance party" at the end of class; a quick whip around the room to thank another person for his or her contribution; a final (postreflection) review of "things we did well" formed via

Figure 5.10   Framework for Next Generation Instruction: Exclaiming

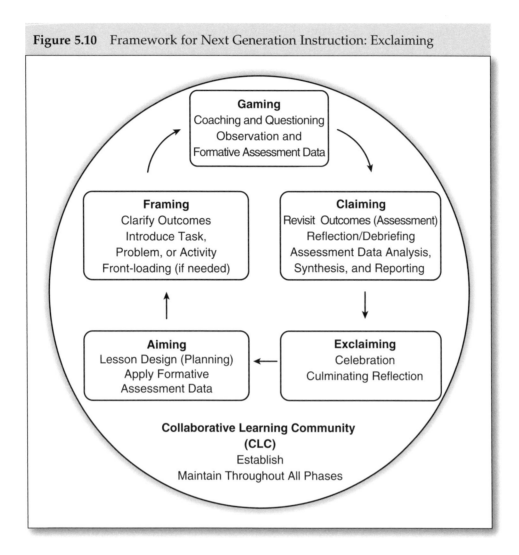

small-group discussion, recorded on sticky notes, and shared aloud—each of these can create a sense of collaborative success and mutually supported satisfaction. This isn't a time to reopen the full reflection process. Rather it's a time to "hit the high points (and the hard parts)" and briefly review the aspects of the learning experience that were most powerful for the group as a whole. Mostly, though, it's a time to celebrate the hard work, the learning that's taken place, and the completion of the experience.

The Otter Valley team say they work to

create opportunities to share and publicize students' work. We often reward success by giving students more responsibility/challenges. We celebrate and reflect on their growth and the milestones they have met (first final exam, first presentation, etc.), and we do our best to establish a culture of being proud of hard work done and pride in perseverance. We try to communicate with parents when students have successes, not just when they struggle.

Jenn takes a similar tack:

> Students are celebrated publicly and in private. I try to make a point of calling home or sending an e-mail with good news about a student. Parents (especially of teenagers) are usually very appreciative of learning about anything that is going on in their child's life. It's nice for a parent to get a phone call from a school that doesn't start with "It's not an emergency, but I would like to talk with you about an incident that occurred today." You should make a big deal over progress. Students get excited by seeing you get excited. A little praise can go a long way.

Louise adds, "First off, I laugh with them a lot. It sounds funny, but that really lets them know you appreciate their everyday world."

6

Tips, Activities, and Tools for Next Generation Instruction

Gaming, Claiming, and Exclaiming

Whatever you do, or dream you can, begin it. Boldness has genius and power and magic in it.

—Johann Wolfgang von Goethe

When guiding students in the Gaming, Claiming, and Exclaiming phases, even the novice facilitator can apply a few simple techniques immediately:

- Ask carefully phrased, specific, concrete, open-ended questions. Don't ask, "How do you think we did?" which begs the reply "Fine," or "Good." Instead ask your students, "What did we do well?" or "What did you do first?" or "How could we have done that differently?" Start with *Why, How, What,* and *What if.*

- Stick to one concept at a time and emphasize clarity over complexity. Decide before you move into the reflection process exactly what you want to pinpoint, be it communication skills, self-management, or use of materials. Once you've determined that, don't let the reflection veer off into a different area unless you're absolutely sure you should. ("I really appreciate that point. How were we better communicators because of that?" "Tell me more about how that ties into our goal to _____.")
- Make notes both during the activity and during the debriefing so that you don't forget the key points you want to touch upon—but don't feel that you have to hit every single piece every single time.
- It is important to recognize that there are many tools beyond writing available for reflection. Some of these include discussion, role-playing, drawing, playing music, and using different technologies.
- Sit in a circle to allow for good hearing and eye contact. Don't let students sit with their backs to each other or sit behind one another, even if this means having them pull chairs away from their desks or push desks around. You may need to rethink your room arrangement in order to facilitate this.
- Pay attention to body language—yours as well as your students'. Sometimes "closed body language" is about external factors such as hunger, drafts in the room, etc. But sometimes it's about discomfort with conversation. Watch for patterns and adjust accordingly.
- Maintain a safe and supportive atmosphere. This means being very careful about the words you use, whom you affirm during discussion, and how you construct groups. It may also mean making adjustments midstream in order to keep students feeling safe and challenged.
- Set ground rules—your Full-Value Contract/Class Expectations—and really use them. Following are some examples:
  - Speak for oneself.
  - One person talks at a time.
  - Listen and talk in the here and now about the work we've been doing together.
  - Respect self, others, and the environment.
  - Maintain the right to pass.
  - Welcome all points of view.
  - Agree/disagree with the idea and not the person.
  - Avoid putdowns.
- Facilitate within your ability. Be reflective about your own growth and experiences and set reasonable goals for yourself. Even something as simple as making the intentional choice to turn more questions back to students can be a great start.

- Explain and revisit the difference between task and process goals. Be sure that students know you're watching for both what they know and how they work.
- When debriefing, progress from positive topics ("What worked well for us?) to negative ("What was hard? What should we try to do differently next time?"). End on a positive note ("What was your favorite part of this challenge?")
- Be clear and concise by having clarity in your expectations and goals *before* you begin.
- Ask one question at a time and give students time to think about their answers. Long pauses (especially after a flurry of answers) mean that people are thinking. Don't be afraid of the quiet.
- Listen to answers and paraphrase to confirm and clarify intent. Restate what you think a student said and model making connections between comments.
- Acknowledge and validate all responses verbally ("Thank you.") or nonverbally (nod).
- Invite quiet students into the conversation by asking them to contribute by name, but don't put anyone on the spot. Use your judgment to determine whom to call on and when. Otherwise, a generic "Does anyone have anything to add?" or a "Turn to a partner and discuss____," can suffice.
- Ask what others think. Encourage differences of opinion.
- Politely interrupt lengthy speakers: Excuse yourself and explain why you are interrupting. Ask, "What about those of you who haven't spoken yet? What do you think?"
- Call a time-out if things seem to be falling apart. Ask the students what they see and hear and whether it lines up with what they are supposed to be doing. Clarify expectations and, if necessary, move to a different activity until you have time to reflect on what went wrong.
- Sometimes students will fail. When that happens, focus on process and next steps rather than the failure itself.
- Stay positive.

ACTIVITIES AND TOOLS FOR GAMING, CLAIMING, AND EXCLAIMING

Remember that Next Generation instruction is a skill that is developed by both teachers and learners. With practice, students will become more comfortable if Claiming activities are thoughtfully sequenced from the concrete (What I did) to the evaluative (How it worked) to the predictive (What I would do differently next time). Whether you have years of experience in the classroom or are brand-new to teaching, in your journey to

Next Generation Instruction, you will face challenging moments that leave you longing for tools. Our colleagues at the American Youth Foundation have provided us with a beginner's list of successful activities that might prove helpful.

- **One-Word Whip.** This is a simple way to start a group and get students comfortable with talking. Ask for a one-word reaction to the activity. Remember always to give students the opportunity to pass.
- **Fist to Five.** With their eyes closed, students need to hold up a fist or any number of fingers of one hand to identify how they feel about a certain question (e.g., How well did we do on our goal to communicate better?). Ask follow-up questions regarding the different opinions.
- **Postcards, Emotion Cards.** Lay out a set of picture cards in the middle of the circle. (Greeting cards, postcards, or pictures cut from magazines are ideal for this activity.) Ask participants to pick a card that represents how they feel about the day, the lesson, the group, their personal role in the group, a strength, area of growth, etc.
- **Concentric Circles.** Create an inner and outer circle of participants. Pairs can quickly answer a question that the facilitator asks about the activity the group is processing. It can be less threatening for participants to speak to one person at a time than to express opinions to the whole group. Inner or outer circles move on to the next person for each question, making the activity feel safe due to the brief contact each student has with another. At the end, you may choose to ask students to share something they heard or said with the entire class.
- **Dyads and Triads.** Students are sent off in groups of two or three to reflect together on the experience. Reflection can be done through predetermined questions, a mapping assignment (see below), or an unstructured conversation.
- **Skills List.** In dyads or triads, students brainstorm a list of skills used in an activity. Then they create a sentence describing how they might apply one or more skills to a real-life situation, which they present to the larger group.
- **Found Objects.** Each group member picks an object in the room that represents how he or she felt about the experience.
- **Fish Bowling.** Split the group into two and form circles; the outer circle observes the inner circle's discussion. Have students share observations.
- **Ball of String (aka Spider Web).** Toss the ball of string with the tail unraveling from speaker to speaker. Identify patterns. Who talked? Who didn't talk? What does that tell us?

- **Shared Learning Circle.** The leader begins by explaining that this circle is a sharing opportunity for group members and then asks everyone to complete a given statement according to their feelings or thoughts.

  Examples:

  > *One thing I appreciate about myself is . . .* or *One thing I appreciate about the person to my right is . . .*
  >
  > *I thought it was neat because I felt . . .*
  >
  > *The feeling today that I would most like to share is . . .*
  >
  > *I felt most proud today about . . .*

- **Mapping.** This can serve as a final closing and transfer activity. Students identify a road map that includes where they started, what their journey has been like (challenges, obstacles, learning, highlights) and where they are going next (goals, hopes, action steps).
- **Journaling.** Students can do a freewriting activity or answer specific reflection questions. This can be a good activity for a class that has become overly boisterous or noisy and needs a calming, centering experience.
- **Letter to Self.** Give the class about 20–30 minutes to write a letter to self, which will remain confidential (provide envelopes). Collect the letters and hand them out later in the year or at the beginning of the following year. The focus can be on "a goal you have for this year," "something you learned about yourself," "something you learned about your classmates," "something that challenged you," or "a goal for yourself for the next school year."
- **Compass Points (aka North-South-East-West).** Ask students to break into groups according to the "direction" that best describes their working style or that they feel best represents their initial thoughts when given a new task.

  North. Do it now. Get it done.
  South. How is everyone feeling? Let's share, support, and connect.
  East. I want to envision, express, and imagine.
  West. Who, what, when, where, how?

  Each group should answer the following questions together:

  > What are four strengths of our style?
  >
  > What are four limitations of our style?
  >
  > What kind of people—from the north, south, east, or west—do we have the most difficulty working with? Why?
  >
  > What would we like others to know about our style?

Have the groups present their answers. Ask students to make a note of their direction and refer to that when breaking into new groups that are not sorted by direction. Then have them explore their styles in more depth by discussing these questions:

What would happen if a group had too many of one direction or another?

What would happen if a group didn't have enough Norths? Souths? Wests? Easts?

What if our group didn't have anyone from a particular direction—how could we compensate?

7

Assessment

You're a good learner—and here's how I know.

—QED Foundation

"How'm I doin'?"
"Am I done yet?"
"Why'd you give me a C?"

Classroom teachers are intimately familiar with not only these but hundreds of other requests for assessment from students. Frustrating to no end, the requests seem to come after multiple explanations of the assignment, review of the homework, and description of how the grade will be assigned—or was assigned. They drive us to distraction, forcing us to wonder what language our students must be hearing when we speak, since they obviously haven't understood a word we're saying.

Needless to say, it bothers us.

So how can we "do" assessment better? How can we assess on the fly, making assessment a part of our day-to-day routine rather than an albatross dangling from our already tension-filled necks? How can assessment coexist with the collaborative learning communities that we work so hard to create? Is it oxymoronic to talk about collaboration and community in the same breath as assessment? How do we assess in such a way that our students see assessment as an expression of our respect for them, rather than as a bludgeon used to beat the joy out of any learning that might take place? For most of us, the word *assessment* brings to mind visions of paper and pencils; true/false, multiple-choice, fill-in-the-blank (with or without a word bank), and essay exams; and standardized tests with their little bubbles and directions to "read this passage and answer the questions." Assessment is the thing that happens that gives us a grade, the thing we use to give our students a grade, at the end of a unit or a chapter or a week. It's how we know how we did, right?

> ❝ From my perspective, the fundamental purpose of assessment is to give students *feedback* to help them learn.   ❞

The term *assessment* has many meanings. It can refer to grading work, sorting students, reporting to parents, identifying strengths and weaknesses, diagnosing problems, being accountable to the system, and so on. Rarely does one assessment strategy meet all these diverse purposes. From my perspective, the fundamental purpose of assessment is to give students *feedback* to help them learn.

Assessment has three purposes. The first is what we all remember: It's the measure of how much we know at a certain moment in time. When it's a final measure, given at the end of instructional activities, it's a *summative* assessment. It is used to justify the grade given or the placement in the next course. It is an "assessment of learning" (Ainsworth & Viegut, 2006).

Alternatively, when we use assessment at the beginning or middle of the instructional process, it becomes "assessment for learning" (Ainsworth & Viegut, 2006), measuring whether our students know what we need them to know at this point in the lesson and helping us to determine what to do next. It is this *formative* assessment that is often given short shrift in the day-to-day work of teaching. Many teachers do this instinctively, but rare is the K–12 educator who is intentional in its use.

Assessments of all types can be *norm referenced* (based on how a student performs in comparison to peers) or *criterion referenced* (based on how many items a student answers correctly in comparison to the number of possible correct items). In the case of the latter, all students may demonstrate the same level of proficiency—everyone can get an A. In the former, there will be a range of grades, which may or may not fall along a bell curve. The purposes of the two types are simple: The first provides a clear picture of who knows the most, who knows the least, and who is in the middle—at least inasmuch as any single moment in time can tell us that. The second tells how much how much the students know. Period.

The normative nature of some exams connects us to the earliest purpose of assessment: to sort the educational wheat from the chaff so that only those perceived as most likely to succeed had access to advanced learning. We know now, however, that most early (and many current) norm-referenced exams are filled with bias and may measure a student's affluence or mother's educational level more accurately than the student's potential. Most teachers understand this (though many political leaders fail to) and try to take all kinds of data into account when determining what a student knows, doesn't know, and needs to know or do next.

I teach a graduate-level course in assessment each year. It is usually made up of about 10 experienced teachers and 10 preservice teachers. Inevitably, the conversation ends up on two tracks. Experienced teachers wish to explore and discover new ways to assess more accurately. Inexperienced teachers want to understand how to use traditional measures; that is, they want to learn how to write a multiple-choice test. To both the experienced and novice teachers reading this, let me offer this advice:

If you understand what you're looking for, you'll inevitably discover the correct route to find it. If you don't know what you're looking for, you'll never find anything.

In short, students need to know what is expected, what they did well and what they need to improve upon (and how to do so), and where they are in relation to learning standards. A single composite grade rarely serves as adequate feedback to students. Effort, achievement, progress, presentation, content, work process, and teacher's feelings about a student all get lumped into one score. The problem isn't grades themselves but having too few grades that aren't specific in terms of what they mean.

> 66 Where do we want our students to be at the end of the lesson, the day, the week, or the year? What do we need them to know, do, and be like if they are to succeed both in and out of school? Answering these questions can be time-consuming, but the wise educator realizes that this time is well spent. 99

In looking at our practice as Next Generation instructors, we must begin by asking ourselves where we want to end up—a key element of the Aiming phase. Where do we want our students to be at the end of the lesson, the day, the week, or the year? What do we need them to know, do, and be like if they are to succeed both in and out of school? Answering these questions can be time-consuming, but the wise educator realizes that this time is well spent. It provides a road map for planning, helping us to sort the essential learnings (of both content and process) from the flashy, fun, kid-friendly stuff that can steal our focus. This is not to imply that good teaching is neither flashy nor fun nor kid friendly—in many cases it is all three. We must clarify, however, that the techniques we use to teach our lessons (the projects, activities, units, and challenges) are the *means* to learning the content and skills rather than an end unto themselves.

From the moment you make your expectations clear while Framing, through your observations and feedback in the Gaming and Claiming phases, right up to your planning in the next round of Aiming, assessment is a thread running right alongside instruction. Meaningful assessment is intended for meaningful tasks. An investment of an hour to assess a student task that took five minutes is neither practical nor appropriate. If students are engaged in meaningful work, however, you will want to make the worthwhile investment of time it takes to provide meaningful feedback.

Meaningful feedback is based on conceiving of assessment as a process, not an event. Assessment is more than endpoint evaluation. The key concept is *evidence*—that is, what we look for students to make or do to demonstrate that they have achieved a desired result. Evidence can and should be collected throughout the instructional process.

Coming from the Latin root *ad sedere* meaning "to sit beside," assessment done well provides us with a set of tools and strategies to get to know our students more fully and, thus, better meet their needs on a day-to-day basis. When effective, assessment gives us a window into the ever-changing landscape of our students' understanding. Done poorly, it can waste important resources, including time, money, and energy—none of which we have to spare.

We can gather assessment data in unintentional, informal, formal ways. We need to give consideration to all three kinds in the classroom: Address the unintentional through a supportive classroom culture, the informal through the development of coaching schemes, and the formal through a quality approach to assessment. In the classroom, feedback comes from multiple sources—self-reflection, peers, teachers, and perhaps the larger community (McGrath, 2007). For Jenn Huard,

> it is very important to preassess so you know where students are to begin with and then to do formative assessments along the way. If students are missing a concept, we need to go back and reteach it in a different manner. For summative assessments, I tend to not like standard tests and quizzes, as I prefer using more creative, authentic assessments. Offering choice benefits the student. Students should always have checklists, rubrics, and models to help them meet the requirements of an assignment. Also, with summative assessments, it is critical that if students have not mastered concepts that you feel are critical, you provide time to look at mistakes and make corrections or even to reteach. We are teachers, and our goal is to have students learn, so it is important to invest in that learning. Even when we feel we did everything possible and the students did not put in the effort necessary, we should evaluate what we are asking for and the process that we used to get there. If the goal is learning and that is not happening, you need to ask yourself what you can do to help all students learn.

But sometimes we lose sight of exactly what students are supposed to be learning—and what we are supposed to be assessing. Remember Quinn's six questions (Quinn, n.d.) from Chapter 3?

1. What am I teaching?

2. Why am I teaching it?

3. How am I teaching it?

4. Why am I teaching it that way?

5. How do I know my kids are getting it?

6. How do the kids know they are getting it?

Let's look at these questions again through a slightly different lens. I love *The Haunting of Hill House* by Shirley Jackson. I've always loved it, ever since I read it in Ms. Throckmorton's 10th-grade English class. It is a masterwork of suspense, and, frankly, it gives me the heeby-est of jee-bies. I always taught it in October because it's a good, scary read and because it's thematic and because I love it. When I first taught English and I filled out my plan book, I wrote "Hill House" across the whole month of October. I had discussion questions about plot, about symbolism, about the historical context, and about theme. When my peers asked me what I was teaching, I answered "Hill House." Simple, right?

> 66 The summative assessment reflected my own lack of clarity around what the content was that I was teaching. 99

Not so much. My love of *Hill House* had blinded me to the reality that *Hill House,* wonderful as it is, is only a means to an end. While I would love to believe that my students are equally enamored of the work, in reality they often don't get it. Their responses to my traditionally written final exams usually reflected a surface-level understanding of the plot (at best) and some superficial awareness of the themes that I had told them existed in the book. The summative assessment reflected my own lack of clarity around what the content was that I was teaching through the medium of *The Haunting of Hill House.* Going back to Quinn's six questions, however, helped me to gain the clarity I lacked and move toward better assessment (and instruction).

Question 1. I immediately had to change the answer to question 1 from *"The Haunting of Hill House"* to "literary devices and elements of plot." This pointed me toward the formative and summative assessments that I'd be working with (since I already had assessments that I use to measure understanding of these ideas in other contexts), as well as the methods that I'd need to use to scaffold instruction. These would, in turn, drive my day-to-day planning.

Question 2. The answer here changed from "Because I love it—it's a great book, plus it's Halloween!" to "These are the state-approved Grade Span Expectations for 10th-grade English" (now I would point to their alignment with the Common Core State Standards) and "My peers expect 11th graders to know these two things."

Question 3. This was just plain embarrassing. How was I teaching it? "We read aloud in class because I don't believe anyone will read it for homework [ouch!]. I ask questions, which, after a long pause, I answer."

This obviously was not an answer I could let stand. How will I teach it? I'll begin with a seminar on what scares us, exploring the concept of fear from a lot of different perspectives. I'll use a challenge in which I ask kids to write and/or tell scary stories (urban legends or campfire ghost stories, maybe?), which we'll dissect for plot elements and maybe for literary devices. I'll do more with kinesthetic methods like plot mapping and character-sketch carousels. I'll create challenges that ask students to evaluate characters in relation to one another and to decide whether the book is really as scary as I think it is.

Question 4. I'll teach it that way because it's a better way to get my kids engaged in the story. I still believe that, if I can get them hooked, they'll like it. My job is to get them hooked on the story.

Questions 5 and 6. The last two questions, "How do I know my kids are getting it?" And "How do the kids know they are getting it?" are where the assessments live. I'll know my kids are getting it when they can identify allusion, alliteration, simile, metaphor, and onomatopoeia in the context of the story and explain why they make the story more effective—or why they don't. The kids will know they're getting it by tracking the results of their formative assessments, which ask them to identify examples of different literary devices from that day's reading and/or discussion. They'll chart which devices they've identified correctly, how many times they've identified them correctly, and which ones are still confusing. I'll also use end-of-day (EOD) sheets (Figure 7.1), asking students to reflect on their process and understanding each day. The accumulated EOD sheets will give the kids evidence and examples they can use to produce a final reflection paper on the process of reading the book and their understanding of the elements of plot and the literary devices that we've studied.

> **❝** Quality criteria are the specifics. They are the individual ideas, qualities, and characteristics that we look or listen for in the products students create and in the processes they use to create them. **❞**

After just a quick walk through the six questions, I have a solid sense of where I'm going with this unit, and I have some techniques in place to help me measure whether my kids understand—before we get to the summative assessment!

The questions you answered for yourself in the Aiming phase (and communicated clearly to your students in Framing) are the same questions that will serve you in your assessment of student learning in the Claiming phase. *Quality criteria* are one way to turn the answers to your Aiming questions into useful tools for students. Quality criteria are the specifics. They are the individual ideas, qualities, and characteristics that we look or listen for in the products students create

Figure 7.1 Example End-of-Day Sheet

End-of-Day Sheet

Name: _____

Class: _____

Date: _____

Please write your thoughts on at least three of the following questions:

> What I learned was . . .
>
> What I found interesting about this work was . . .
>
> What surprised me was . . .
>
> I want to know more about . . .
>
> Right now I'm feeling . . .
>
> This experience might have been more valuable to me if . . .

Source: McGrath, 2010. Used with permission.

and in the processes they use to create them. They are the observable behaviors that show students have an understanding of the concepts and issues central to the work they are doing and that they are gaining command of vital skills and dispositions. Quality criteria provide a real-world reflection of what is "top-notch" and what is "bottom-drawer."

We all unconsciously apply some standard regarding what quality means in our daily lives. Does this soup taste really good, or is it barely edible? Is this essay publishable? Is this music worth listening to? We make decisions every day based on our internal criteria. Yet, in all likelihood, we are not consciously articulating our quality criteria as we make those decisions. We simply "know." We could with some effort list the qualities of the soup, the essay, or the music that make it worthy. But how did we come to know this? Our internal quality criteria were largely developed through a lengthy process of experience and a good deal of feedback from our environment—including feedback from our interaction with others.

We can and do develop our internal quality measures without consciously reflecting on them, but if we don't periodically check our reference points, we risk perpetuating misconceptions and poor judgment. The process of reflecting on quality—bringing our criteria to a conscious level to be explored and examined—has the potential to facilitate, develop, and hone our internal quality system. What is good? Why is it good? How will we know? Do we all agree? For the Otter Valley team, this means collaborating on a number of different rubrics—schoolwide writing and communication rubrics and rubrics designed specifically for certain projects—as well as creating and using formative assessments and then checking in with one another about the results. The team members engage in collaborative processes daily using formal planning time as well as informal conversations in order to most effectively revise or revamp their approach.

> **❝** Quality Criteria, used well, can help you overcome unintended bias based on cultural expectations or relative affluence and will help your students be exactly as successful as they wish to be. **❞**

Quality criteria answer obvious (but often unstated) questions for students: When I do this work, what does excellence look/sound/feel like? What is a good or fair effort? What falls short of the mark? To be successful, students need to know the answers. If we put the answer out on the table in the classroom, we will all know what we are aiming for (McGrath, 2007). Good quality criteria can help you zero in on the things that matter most to you and will prevent you from being distracted by beautiful (or less than) products that fail to demonstrate the content or that show extraordinary (or less than) creativity or parental support. Quality criteria, used well, can help you overcome unintended bias based on cultural expectations or relative affluence and will help your students be exactly as successful as they wish to be. The box "Setting Quality Criteria: A Procedure" describes one way of creating concrete, observable descriptions of the form, content, and process(es) you wish to assess.

BOX 7.1   SETTING QUALITY CRITERIA: A PROCEDURE

1. Be clear about what kinds of quality criteria are being set:
   - Content knowledge
   - Process skills/behaviors (e.g., collaboration, communication)

2. Determine how quality criteria will be set:
   a. Established by you.
   b. Negotiated with students with your facilitation.
   c. Set by students alone.

Regardless of how final criteria will be set, create a basic set of quality criteria, even if it will ultimately be for your use only.

3. Give consideration to the following:

- **Form criteria**. What characteristics are essential to quality in the product's form or structure? (Examples: The poster is large enough to be easily seen from a distance of 10 feet. The paper is 5 pages long and double-spaced. The presentation lasts 3 minutes and has a visual aid.)

- **Content criteria**. What characteristics are essential to a representation of quality content? The focus here is on exhibitions of knowledge and understanding. (Examples: The poster conveys all the key relationships of the water cycle. The paper includes the key events from *The Taming of the Shrew*. The experiment demonstrates the effect of mass on acceleration. The model shows the relationship between a square and rhombus.)

- **Process criteria**. What observable behaviors are essential to quality work in a skill or dispositional area? (e.g., documenting an orderly plan to attack the problem, taking turns speaking, asking probing questions about others' ideas, organizing materials over a multi-day project) What do you want to see students doing while they are working?

4a. Present your quality criteria to the students, using a list you've created.

or

4b. Negotiate quality criteria with students.

   a. Give students models of real-world products. Ask them to identify quality characteristics of the product and of the process that they infer was used to create it. (*Note:* Be cautious when providing examples, as students may replicate the models rather than creating original work. Either provide a very diverse set or show the exemplars with the caveat that students may not duplicate them.)

   b. Use language that makes it clear that quality work and processes are the goal that underlies criteria setting.

   c. Guide students in the brainstorming of criteria.

   d. Cull, combine, and modify criteria, striving for a set that is truly indicative of quality.

   e. Participate in this process, adding your own criteria as appropriate.

or

4c. Allow students to set their own quality criteria. They can meet with you to sign off on these criteria.

(Continued)

(Continued)

5. As students engage in work on the challenge, refocus their attention on the criteria.
   - "How does the approach that you are taking here relate to the criteria that have been set?"
   - "Does this decision represent a compromise on quality?"
   - "Is this quality characteristic working for you? Should we modify it?"

6. Hold students accountable to their quality criteria.
   - Use the criteria as the basis for assessing student work, as well as for giving both summative and formative feedback.
   - Use process criteria during midprocess and final debriefings to help students reflect on their work habits and make plans for future work.

7. Convert the quality criteria into an assessment rubric.

8. Have students self-assess against their quality criteria using the rubric.

9. Avoid the pitfall of using criteria as "minimum expectations for a grade." If an item is not included in the quality criteria, it cannot be used to raise or lower a student's grade.

Source: Adapted from McGrath, 2007.

The time previously spent running in circles, answering every question (many more than once), finding and allocating resources, and driving the learning in your classroom will now be spent in coaching and observation of not just your students' new understanding of content but also their growing process skills required by the Common Core and Inquiry. Figures 7.3–7.13 show some examples of tools created by Allison Robinson, Al Magnusson, and the team from Otter Valley Union for documenting and assessing process and product quality criteria.

This elegant trade-off is the most valuable aspect of instructional facilitation:

Instructional facilitation → More time for observation of students at work

More time for observation → Better data about what students know and can do

Better data collection → Meaningful, timely formative assessment

Meaningful, timely formative assessment → Immediate support in areas of need

Immediate support in areas of need → Improved student success

By becoming a coach rather than being the sole source of information in your classroom, you will have time to see what your students know and can do. In other words, you'll have more time for meaningful assessment. With your knowledge of your students' learning, you'll be able to adjust expectations, refine behavior, and remediate content knowledge on the spot.

Now that you have the time to give immediate feedback—to let students know your perceptions of and feelings about their behaviors and progress—it's important to be clear about how you will give this feedback. You can use the guidelines in Figure 7.2 to craft language that is helpful, effective, and success oriented. The goal is to help the student imagine a different set of choices by outlining expectations that can be reinforced; in this way, behavior that is hurtful, uncooperative, and self-defeating can be changed. Share your expectations with your students either separately or by making them part of your Full-Value Contract/Class Expectations.

Many classroom facilitators will find that they struggle with assessment. Typically, this struggle is rooted in too much information rather than too little. Good observation will provide you with a lot of information about what your students know and can do, and clarity around what you're looking for will make it easier to decide what to record and what to simply notice.

(Text continued on page 124)

Figure 7.2 Guidelines for Giving and Receiving Feedback

Giving Feedback

Be clear and specific.

Describe the behavior observed and the behavior expected.

Don't evaluate the person. Instead discuss the behavior.

Be direct and sincere.

Use good timing—the sooner after the behavior, the better.

Use *I* statements.

Receiving Feedback

Try to understand.

Ask for clarification.

Focus on the behavior, not on the person giving the feedback ("Don't kill the messenger").

Check your perceptions against those of other group members.

You have the choice to accept or to reject feedback.

Figure 7.3 Example Leadership Checklist

Leadership Checklist

Name _____   Class _____

Leadership: A skill with which a person can use a process to help and guide others in a certain task.

  Characteristics for this life skill or behavior are listed on the left side of this chart. Use the following rating system to evaluate how you think your leadership was for the activity designated by your teacher.

  OUT = Outstanding   (Fantastic)

  COM = Competent   (Very Good)

  ACC = Acceptable   (Fair)

  NW = Needs Work   (Needs Improvement)

  N/A = Not Available   (Does Not Apply)

Activities, Classroom Lessons, Dates, Length of Time, etc. (Write sideways.)

Leadership Characteristics								
I often try to be a positive leader in school, in class, and in groups.								
I challenge myself to find ways to help others in school, in class, and in group work.								
In groups I help others see what needs to be done.								
I sometimes do certain things around the classroom to help the class run smoothly.								
I help other kids if they do not understand.								

I try to be consistently responsible.							
I am trying to improve my personal responsibility.							
I can help people get along.							
I can do my work without making problems for other kids or the teacher.							
When in a group, I try to guide others to do their best, not boss them around.							
I am polite and respectful of my classmates' different abilities.							
I enjoy doing the highest-quality work possible.							
I work hard to have good self-direction.							
I try to be organized all the time.							
I have high expectations for myself.							
I can "step up" and take charge in a constructive way.							
When there are many different ideas, I can help others find a common idea to work with.							
I see that it is important to value everyone's idea.							
If I am not the leader, I can follow others' directions to make the process go smoothly.							

Comments:

Figure 7.4   Example Organization Checklist

Organization Checklist

Name _____   Class _____

Organization: A skill by which a student actively tries his or her best to sequence and arrange things properly in terms of the task being worked on or, in other words, by which the student tries to productively manage time, space, materials, and tasks.

Characteristics for this life skill or behavior are listed on the left side of this chart. Use the following rating system to evaluate how you think your organization was for the activity designated by your teacher.

OUT = Outstanding   (Fantastic)

COM = Competent   (Very Good)

ACC = Acceptable   (Fair)

NW = Needs Work   (Needs Improvement)

N/A = Not Available   (Does Not Apply)

Activities, Classroom Lessons, Dates, Length of Time, etc. (Write sideways.)

Organization Characteristics								
I was able to make the bigger task(s) into smaller tasks.								
I used my time well.								
I did the best I could with the resources and space available.								
I tried to manage the details without getting upset.								

I know that sometimes I have to take care of unexpected details that come up.								
I may have used tools to help keep things in order: rubric, checklist, rough drafts, etc.								
I can see what is important and write it down in my own words.								
I used a mental timeline or one on paper to help get the task(s) completed.								
I understand that proper organizing can help me be more productive and more successful.								
If there were any problems, I tried to work them out in a peaceful way.								
I know it's important to work on having a systematic mind-set.								
I know to ask a classmate or teacher for help if I get stuck.								
Overall organization.								
Comments:								

Figure 7.5   Example Self-Direction Checklist

Self-Direction Checklist

Name _____   Class _____

Self-Direction: A behavior by which a person actively thinks about managing himself or herself in a positive manner and makes a strong effort to do well at the assigned task. Self-direction can apply when a person does independent work or when he or she works with others to maximize the collaborative effort.

Characteristics for this life skill or behavior are listed on the left side of this chart. Use the following rating system to evaluate how you think your self-direction was for the activity designated by your teacher.

OUT = Outstanding   (Fantastic)

COM = Competent   (Very Good)

ACC = Acceptable   (Fair)

NW = Needs Work   (Needs Improvement)

N/A = Not Available   (Does Not Apply)

Activities, Classroom Lessons, Dates, Length of Time, etc. (Write sideways.)

Self-Direction Characteristics								
Look at new things in class as an interesting challenge.								
Work in class at a reasonable noise level.								
Be serious about trying to do well in class.								
Use good manners.								
Listen well to teacher.								

Listen well to class members.									
Use safe actions.									
Attempt to stay on-task 85 percent of the time.									
Try hard to do quality work.									
Walk (not run) in the classroom.									
Attempt to follow rules.									
Comments:									

Figure 7.6   Example Collaboration Checklist

Collaboration Checklist

Name _____   Class _____

Collaboration: A behavior by which a student tries his or her best to do a fair share of the group's work, takes full advantage of teamwork, is supportive in the group, and attempts to get the most out of the group situation.

    Characteristics for this life skill or behavior are listed on the left side of this chart. Use the following rating system to evaluate how you think your collaboration was for the activity designated by your teacher.

    OUT = Outstanding   (Fantastic)

    COM = Competent   (Very Good)

    ACC = Acceptable   (Fair)

    NW = Needs Work   (Needs Improvement)

    N/A = Not Available   (Does Not Apply)

Activities, Classroom Lessons, Dates, Length of Time, etc. (Write sideways.)

(Continued)

Figure 7.6 (Continued)

Collaboration Characteristics							
I know that working in groups is necessary in life.							
I understand what needed to be done.							
I checked that everyone else knew what to do.							
I used good manners.							
I was completely (85%) involved in the group process.							
I listened well to class members.							
I know that "storming" is part of the development of collaboration.							
I helped the group work in a positive manner.							
I offered productive ideas/information to the group.							
I stood up for my idea(s) when they were different than the group's.							
My positive self-direction helped the process go smoothly.							
I did *not* sabotage the group process.							

Personal issues did not take away from the group process.							
I helped work out problems in a peaceful, productive manner.							
I knew my job and worked well to get it done.							
I gave compliments.							
Opinion of overall group collaboration							
Comments:							

Figure 7.7   Example Checklist Rubric for Product Quality

Checklist Rubric for Product Quality

Please list the group members: *Michael, Bethany, James, and Amber*

Please indicate your assessment of the product:

Form

1. Colorful   (definitely)   I think so   not yet   NA

2. Organized   definitely   I think so   not yet   NA

3. Neat   (definitely)   I think so   not yet   NA

4. Creative   (definitely)   I think so   not yet   NA

Content/Information

1. Did we answer the questions?   (definitely   I think so)   not yet   NA

2. Use specific details?   (definitely   I think so)   not yet   NA

3. Provide accurate information?   definitely   (I think so)   not yet   NA

4. Use correct grammar?   definitely   (I think so)   not yet   NA

Some errors.

(Continued)

Figure 7.7 (Continued)

Process

1. Use time wisely?	⟨definitely	I think so⟩	not yet	NA
2. Divide workload evenly?	⟨definitely⟩	I think so	not yet	NA
3. Stay on-task?	⟨definitely⟩	I think so	not yet	NA
4. Accomplish goals?	definitely	⟨I think so⟩	not yet	NA

Overall Comments

It was a good group to work with, but I felt as though two of us had to put in a lot more time than the others, which can become frustrating! Next time we need to do a better job of dividing up the work.

Source: Critical Skills Program, 2009. Used with permission.

Figure 7.8   Example Challenge Feedback

Challenge Feedback

Student name: Cathy

Challenge: Russian Tourism Bureau

The group's efforts resulted in a product that . . .

- ☑ Exceeded the criteria on the product rubric.
- ☐ Met the criteria on the product rubric.
- ☐ Approached the criteria on the product rubric.
- ☐ Was below the criteria on the product rubric.

Your ownership of the product, as evidence by the quantity and quality of your overall contributions to the process, generally . . .

- ☑ Exceeded the criteria for ownership (above the group's level by +1) = actively engaged, leading and learning, helping others learn, making things happen, *showing clear, explicit understanding of the content.*
- ☐ Met the criteria for ownership (stayed at group's level) or was a solo effort = active most or all of the time; application of content apparent.
- ☐ Approached the criteria for ownership (AC or below the group's level by −1) = some active participation, regularly picked up before the bell, evidence of application of content is slight.
- ☐ Was below the criteria for ownership (BC or below group's level by −2) = a little participation, not interfering, little evidence of understanding.
- ☐ No evidence = absent or not engaged or interfering with others' learning.

[Note: AC = Approached criteria; BC = Below criteria.]

Therefore, as a result of the evidence provided by the group's work and your degree of ownership of the task, the overall evidence of your skills and understanding . . .

☑ Exceeded the criteria.   Comments on skills and understanding . . .

☐ Met the criteria.   *Good job getting detailed, thorough information!*

☐ Approached the criteria.

☐ Was below the criteria.

☐ No evidence

Your particular contributions to the process and/or product . . .

You were a good team member and did a good job ensuring your group had the information it needed.

Process skills and attitudes you demonstrated particularly well:

Great effort, creativity, and thoroughness.

Things to keep in mind for next time:

Continue to be creative!

Source: Critical Skills Program, 2009. Used with permission.

Figure 7.9 Example Oral Communications Rubric

Oral Communications Rubric				
Criteria	Proficient With Distinction	Proficient	Nearly Proficient	Below the Standard
Content: Organization 1%	Explicit introduction, effective transitions, logical conclusion	Adequate introduction, evidence transitions, logical conclusion	Limited introduction, inconsistent transitions or conclusion	Lacks introduction, transitions, or a logical conclusion
Knowledge of Subject 75%	Specific, accurate details; comprehensive explanation	Adequate details and explanation	Uneven use of details or superficial explanation	Lacks details or explanation
Delivery: Enunciation 1%	Clear, consistent pronunciation	Few pronunciation errors	Repeated pronunciation errors	Mispronunciation detracts from speech
Fluency/ Pace 1%	Consistent and appropriate pacing and emphasis	Some inconsistency in pacing and emphasis	Inconsistent pacing and emphasis	Frequent pauses, little or no emphasis, distracts from presentation

(Continued)

Figure 7.9 (Continued)

		Oral Communications Rubric		
Criteria	Proficient With Distinction	Proficient	Nearly Proficient	Below the Standard
Volume 1%	Consistently audible, effective projection	Usually audible, attempts at projection	Inconsistently audible, lapses in projection	Inaudible, feeble attempts at projection
Tonality 1%	Vocal variety, appropriate pitch and inflection	Vocal variety, somewhat effective	Uneven vocal variety	Monotone, no emotion or tone used
Timing 1%	On time	Within 30 seconds	Within 45 seconds	Did not heed time limits at all
Nonverbal: Posture/ Appearance 1%	Effective presence that is suitable for the occasion	Pleasant appearance; confident posture	Distracting posture or appearance	Posture and appearance interfere with effective presentation
Eye Contact 1%	Frequent eye contact, familiarity with script apparent	Occasional eye contact, more reliant upon script	Infrequent eye contact, script often read extensively	Glued to script with little or no eye contact
Props/ Visuals 15%	Integrally incorporated into presentation	Usually incorporated into presentation	Inconsistently incorporated into presentation	Rarely incorporated into presentation
Gestures/ Animation 1%	Consistent body language and facial expression enhance speech	Some body language and facial expressions enhance speech	Infrequent body language and facial expression to enhance speech	Little or no evidence

Source: Otter Valley Union High School Freshman Team. Used with permission.

(Continued)

For example, I may determine that my students need to work on their organization skills and therefore work with them to set clear criteria for organization: What will "organization" look like and sound like while they're working in class? What observable evidence will I be looking for? Over the course of the project, I may notice that students are doing an excellent (or a poor) job of collaborating. I may make note of this and may coach to improve behavior if the lack of skill is preventing students from completing their work, but I won't include that information in my assessments.

Figure 7.10   Example Effort and Participation Rubric

Based on Souhegan High School's Responsible Citizen & Self-Directed Learner Academic Learner Expectations

Criteria	Exceeds Expectations	Meets Expectations	Appoaches Expectations	Does Not Meet Expectations
EFFORT	• Assignments are always on time. • Work is completed to the best of the student's ability and exceeds expectations. • Agenda is always filled in and includes details. • Is always on time & utilizes all time effectively. • Excels when challenged & takes calculated risks.	• Assignments are always on time. • Work is complete and meets expectations. • Agenda is always completed with needed information. • Is always on time and usually uses time effectively. • Accepts challenges & pushes comfortable limits.	• Assignments are almost always handed in on time. • At times, work is incomplete and needs improvement. • Agenda is almost always filled out and never requires more than one cue per week to complete it. • Is late on occasion and does not always use time effectively. • Resists challenges.	• Assignments are frequently handed in late. • Work is often incomplete, and quality does not meet expectations. • Agenda is not always utilized and needs more than one cue per week to fill in agenda. • Is frequently late and usually does not use time effectively. • Gives up when challenged.
CONTRIBUTION	• Always offers ideas and encourages discussions & creates a positive learning environment. • Excellent leadership qualities; goes above and beyond in group work. • Acts as a role model.	• Asks questions in class and offers ideas. • Works well in groups, gets work done, and may serve as a leader. • Supports a positive learning community. • Is almost always respectful of	• Rarely asks questions in groups or offers ideas and discussion points to class. • May not always contribute to groups and does not do fair share of the work. • Sometimes struggles to support a positive	• Impedes the learning of others by distracting with behaviors and comments. • Disrupts group work or does not contribute to the group. • Unwilling or resistant to support the learning community.

(Continued)

Figure 7.10 (Continued)

Criteria	Exceeds Expectations	Meets Expectations	Appoaches Expectations	Does Not Meet Expectations
	• Is always respectful of peers and teacher.	peers and teacher.	learning community. • Occasionally is disrespectful of peers and teachers.	• Interrupts others and is disrespectful to peers or teachers.
ENGAGEMENT	• Always checks work and makes corrections and offers assistance to others. • Actively seeks feedback from teacher and other experts. • Always on-task and redirects others at times. • Always participates in all in class learning opportunities and most out-of-class opportunities when needed (study sessions, academic advisory, etc.).	• Almost always checks work and makes corrections & seeks help to further learning. • Independently obtains feedback and makes changes accordingly. • On-task almost all the time (never requires more than one cue per week to stay on-task). • Participates in all in-class learning opportunities and many out-of-class learning opportunities.	• Usually checks work and usually makes corrections. Needs to ask for further help. • Meets with teacher only when asked. • Off-task to a degree that learning is compromised (more than one cue to remain on task per week is needed). • Participates in learning activities but needs to utilize supports (in-class help, afterschool help or advisory).	• Does not usually check work, make corrections, or seek assistance. • Does not meet with teacher when asked or is expected to. • Is very unfocused & off-task to a degree that the student is unable access information (needs one or more cues per class to stay on-task). • Does not participate in learning opportunities.

Source: Jennifer Huard. Used with permission.

It won't count as part of the grade because I didn't tell students at the outset that I was assessing it. I may choose to bring it up during the debriefing, particularly if students note that they struggled to work together. I may choose to target collaboration next time. I will not, however, lower students' grades or try to gather specific data on collaboration because, simply put, it is not the thing I'm assessing in that lesson. The same goes for content and

(Text continued on page 134)

Figure 7.11 Example Science Progress Report

Hampton Academy

Mr. Alan Magnusson

Science Progress Report

Name _____ Grade _____

Quarter _____ Date _____

This form is to provide the student and his/her parent(s)/guardian(s) with information about the student's progress in science. The form is divided into two parts. One part is a self-evaluation by the student, and the second part is from the teacher. Please discuss the importance of school achievement and success with your son/daughter. If you need additional information, call me at the school (phone #) or contact me through the school's email (email address). This quarter in science, we are learning about

_____

_____

The report uses the following rating scale:

OUT = outstanding; COM = competent, very good; ACC = acceptable, fair; NW = needs work; INC = incomplete; N/A = not available/inapplicable

Student Self-Evaluation

Classwork quality _____   Homework quality _____   Responsibility _____

Organization _____   Working with others _____   Working alone _____

Classwork effort_____   Homework effort_____   Conduct/behavior _____

Participation in class_____   Penmanship_____   Time management_____

Enjoyment of science _____   Overall science success _____   Overall attitude _____

Student's Comments:

Teacher Evaluation

Academics   _____

Effort   _____

Conduct   _____

(Continued)

Figure 7.11 (Continued)

Return only this bottom portion. Cut off at the line and keep the top section.

Parent/Guardian Signature _____

Please have your son/ daughter return by _____

_____

Also . . . please write some comments below . . . from you to your child or from you to me—or a little of both. Thank you!

Comments:

Source: Otter Valley Union High School Freshman Team (Caitlin Steele, Bruce Perlow, Chris Lemieux). Used with permission.

Figure 7.12   Great Aunt Mildred's Space Shot Rubric

Great Aunt Mildred's Space Shot Rubric				
Category	*Excellent*	*Good*	*Satisfactory*	*Poor*
Title	Title tells the type of map and the name of the place and is clearly distinguishable as the title (e.g., larger letters, underlined) and is printed at the top of the map.	Title tells the purpose/content of the map and is printed at the top of the map, but is not clearly distinguishable as the title (e.g., larger letters, underlined) and is printed at the top of the map.	Title is missing the type of map or the name of the place and is not clearly distinguishable as the title (e.g., larger letters, underlined) and is printed at the top of the map.	Title is missing.
Map Legend/Key	Legend is easy to find (clearly defined space) and contains a complete set of symbols.	Legend contains a complete set of symbols but is not easy to find.	Legend contains an almost complete set of symbols and is not easy to find.	Legend is absent or lacks several symbols and is not easy to find.
Scale	The scale used is clearly indicated on the map and	The scale used is clearly indicated on the map but	The scale used is on the map but is not clearly	There is no scale marker on the map.

Category	Excellent	Good	Satisfactory	Poor
	includes the distance.	does not include how distance is measured.	indicated and does not show how distance is measured.	
Compass Rose	The compass rose is clearly indicated on the map, and all cardinal points are labeled.	The compass rose is clearly indicated on the map, and north is labeled.	The compass rose is clearly indicated on the map but does not show where north is.	There is no compass rose on the map.
Type of Map	Only elements of the type of map are present.	Mostly elements of the type of map are present, but there are two to four exceptions.	Few elements of the type of map are present; there are more than four exceptions.	None of the elements of the type of map are present.
Grid	Grid is neatly drawn and evenly spaced. Coordinates are clearly written along at least two edges of the grid.	Grid is neatly drawn and evenly spaced. Coordinates are clearly written along only one edge of the grid.	Grid is neatly drawn and evenly spaced. Coordinates are missing.	No grid is there.
Map Index	Map index is easy to find (clearly defined space) and contains a complete set of coordinates for the major elements of the map.	Map index contains a complete set of coordinates for the major elements of the map but is not easy to find.	Map index contains an almost complete set of coordinates for the major elements of the map and is not easy to find.	Map index is absent or lacks several coordinates for the major elements of the map and is not easy to find.
Quality of Work	Map . . . 1. is of the same place as the other two. 2. is neat and clearly drawn. 3. is well labeled. 4. is without spelling errors.	Map does not meet two of the following: 1. of the same place as the other two 2. neat and clearly drawn 3. well labeled 4. no spelling errors	Map does not meet three of the following: 1. of the same place as the other two 2. neat and clearly drawn 3. well labeled 4. no spelling errors	Map does not meet four or more of the following: 1. of the same place as the other two 2. neat and clearly drawn 3. well labeled 4. no spelling errors

(Continued)

Figure 7.12 (Continued)

Category	Excellent	Good	Satisfactory	Poor
	5. uses capitalization where needed.	5. capitalization where needed	5. capitalization where needed	5. capitalization where needed

Map Type Elements

Political map. It is to be a map of a country. It should have country borders and be divided into smaller political units (states/provinces) and display those borders. It needs to include cities and towns and at least one capital. All places should be given school-appropriate names.

Physical map. At *least* 10 physical features must be indicated, and there must be at least 5 different types of land or water forms represented. All places should be given school-appropriate names.

Special purpose map. The map needs to represent a specific theme and use elements of physical and/or political maps to make it clear.

These are the individual elements that I will be looking for you to demonstrate while working in your groups:

Category	Excellent	Good	Satisfactory	Poor
Problem solving	Actively looks for and suggests solutions to problems.	Refines solutions suggested by others.	Does not suggest or refine solutions, but is willing to try out solutions suggested by others.	Does not try to solve problems or help others solve problems. Lets others do the work.
Creative thinking	Routinely provides useful ideas when participating in the group and in classroom discussion. A definite leader who contributes a lot of effort.	Usually provides useful ideas when participating in the group and in classroom discussion. A strong group member who tries hard!	Sometimes provides useful ideas when participating in the group and in classroom discussion. A satisfactory group member who does what is required.	Rarely provides useful ideas when participating in the group and in classroom discussion. May refuse to participate.
Collaboration	Almost always listens to, shares with, and supports the efforts of others. Tries to keep people working well together.	Usually listens to, shares with, and supports the efforts of others. Does not cause "waves" in the group.	Often listens to, shares with, and supports the efforts of others but sometimes is not a good team member.	Rarely listens to, shares with, and supports the efforts of others. Often is not a good team player.

Source: Allison Robinson. Used with permission.

Figure 7.13   Great Aunt Mildred's U.S. Tour Rubric

Great Aunt Mildred's U.S. Tour Rubric			
Overall Presentation			

0	10	20	
There is no color, you have erase marks and scribbles everywhere, and it looks as if you have dragged it through the mud!	Not too bad, but you did not use much color, and you have stray marks.	Very good job. You have used a variety of color; your papers are neat with no stray marks. Your presentation is excellent.	

Bar Graph			
0	2	6	10
You are missing the graph.	You have the graph, but you did not follow the directions. Your title is incorrect, you do not have the correct labels at the bottom and side, and you do not have equal distances between amount and "stuff." Your bars are not consistent. You have not included all your information.	You have most of your stuff right but not everything. You may have the wrong title or labels, or your distances may not be equal between amount and "stuff." Your bars are not all consistent. You may not have included all your information.	You've got everything right! Your title is correct, you have the correct labels at the bottom and side, and you have equal distances between amount and "stuff." Your bars are all consistent. You have included all your information.

Line Graph			
0	2	6	10
You are missing the graph.	You have the graph, but you did not follow the directions. Your title is incorrect, you do not have the correct labels at the bottom and side, and you do not have equal distances between amount and dates. You have not included all your information and have not drawn the lines correctly.	You have most of your stuff right but not everything. You may have the wrong title or labels, or your distances may not be equal between amount and dates. You may not have included all your information or not drawn your lines correctly.	You've got everything right! Your title is correct, you have the correct labels at the bottom and side, and you have equal distances between amount and dates. You have included all your information and have drawn the lines correctly.

(Continued)

Figure 7.13 (Continued)

Montage			
0	*2*	*6*	*10*
You are missing the graph.	You have the graphic, but you did not follow the directions. Your title is incorrect, and you do not have all your information.	You have most of your stuff right but not everything. You may have the wrong title and/or you do not have all your information.	You've got everything right! Your title is correct, and you have all your information.

Table			
0	*2*	*6*	*10*
You are missing the graph.	You have the graph, but you did not follow the directions. Your title is incorrect; you do not have the correct labels for rows and/or columns. You didn't fill in your table properly.	You have most of your stuff right but not everything. You may have the wrong title, or you do not have the correct labels for rows and/or columns. You may not have filled in your table properly.	You've got everything right! Your title is correct, and you have the correct labels for rows and columns. You have filled in your table properly.

Climagraph			
0	*2*	*6*	*10*
You are missing the graph.	You have the graph, but you did not follow the directions. Your title is incorrect, you do not have the correct labels at the bottom and sides, and you do not have equal distances between amount and dates. You have not included all 12 months. You did not use your line and bar graph properly.	You have most of your stuff right but not everything. You may have the wrong title or labels, or your distances may not be equal between amount and dates. You may not have included all 12 months. You may not have used your line and bar graph properly.	You've got everything right! Your title is correct, you have the correct labels at the bottom and side, and you have equal distances between amount and dates. You have included all 12 months. You used your line and bar graph properly.

Pictograph			
0	*2*	*6*	*10*
You are missing the graph.	You have the graph, but you did not follow the directions. Your title is incorrect; you do not have the correct labels. You do not have a key that contains your picture/symbol and what it is worth. Your pictures/symbols are not consistent.	You have most of your stuff right but not everything. You may have the wrong title, or your key is not complete. Your pictures/symbols may not be consistent.	You've got everything right! Your title is correct, your key is complete, and you have consistent pictures/symbols.

Timeline			
0	*2*	*6*	*10*
You are missing the graph.	You have the graph, but you did not follow the directions. Your title is incorrect; you did not have equal distances between dates. You have not included all information.	You have most of your stuff right but not everything. You may have the wrong title; distances may not be equal between dates. You may not have included information.	You've got everything right! Your title is correct, and you have equal distances between dates. You have included all information.

Circle Graph			
0	*2*	*6*	*10*
You are missing the graph.	You have the graph, but you did not follow the directions. Your title is incorrect, you do not have the correct labels, and your percentages are incorrect and do not add up to 100. You have not included all your information.	You have most of your stuff right but not everything. Your title may not be correct, you do not have the correct labels, or your percentages are incorrect and do not add up to 100. You may not have all your information.	You've got everything right! Your title is correct, you have the correct labels, and your percentages are correct and add up to 100. You have all your information.

(Continued)

Figure 7.13 (Continued)

	Your Points	Possible Points
On Time		0
Overall Presentation		20
Bar Graph		10
Line Graph		10
Pictograph		10
Climagraph		10
Montage		10
Table		10
Timeline		10
Circle Graph		10
TOTAL		100

Source: Allison Robinson. Used with permission.

(Continued)

form criteria: If we assess what we set out to assess—nothing more, nothing less—then we demystify the process for kids, and we simplify our own efforts.

We make choices every day that determine how we will approach assessment and whether it will be a help or a hindrance in our practice. Clarity around what you're evaluating is the key to sorting through the information in order to find what you most need to know in order to plan your next step. This clarity applies not just to you but also to your students. Erin Hunter says,

> For me, the most effective way to assess is to work with the students at the beginning of the unit to create their own standards around process and product and then have them assess themselves using those standards. It's important that they do that for themselves rather than have me do it for them.

If we remain mindful of the power of quality assessment, we will discover we have a powerful resource at our disposal.

8

Conclusion

Every end is a new beginning.

Becoming a facilitative instructor—a Next Generation teacher, prepared not only for the Common Core but also for the inquiry-driven experiences our students need to survive in the 21st century—is a process. It begins with the intentional creation and maintenance of a collaborative learning community. You and your students will commit to pushing beyond the nonproductive collusion that is cooperation to the powerful synergy of collaboration. In order to do so, you must collectively move from a lack (or superficial level) of knowledge about one another via authentic communication. Authentic communication (supported by the classroom teacher through carefully selected tools, activities, and processes) will develop within everyone involved a willingness to trust each other. Once this trust is gained, the teacher can begin to offer content-rich learning experiences, the kind of learning that requires collaboration to maintain a mature learning community.

These well-Aimed learning experiences, grown out of the teacher's clarity around both content standards and the skills and dispositions required by the 21st century, will provide opportunities for students to *engage* with the material in meaningful contexts (Gaming). Via these contexts, they'll *exhibit* their new understanding and *reflect* on the knowledge and skills gained through the experiences (Claiming). The teacher Frames the work to be done and, in the Gaming phrase, shifts from the center of the classroom to be a *coach*. Now the teacher asks more questions than he

Figure 8.1   Framework for Next Generation Instruction: Complete

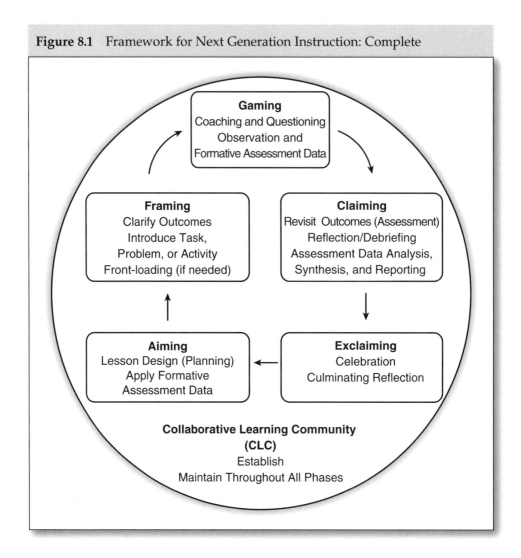

or she answers and provides both *feedback* and *reflection* opportunities as students *exhibit* and Claim their new understanding, providing solid evidence for the teacher to use as formative and summative assessments that are both authentic and valid.

Your capacities as a Next Generation instructor will grow as you continue to use experiential methods that tie content and process together in meaningful contexts and as you shift your perspective from that of "answer giver" to "question asker." Clarity of expectations around the Common Core and what students should know (and how you expect them to demonstrate that knowledge) will support the design of meaningful learning experiences; the creation of reflection opportunities will act as a springboard for new awareness and valid assessment of whether or not students know and can do what they have been taught. You will see the hard work of learning move from your shoulders onto the shoulders of your students, but the load will be lighter there, sparking new energy and enthusiasm on your part as well as theirs.

The shift away from traditional instruction toward Next Generation instruction isn't easy. The status quo has a powerful gravitational pull, and there will be many, many moments when its tug will feel overwhelming. The siren song of "Just do it the way I did it before and see if it works better," will be strong in spite of your awareness that the old way didn't really work very well for all kids—or for you. Give yourself time to take small steps. Then take another step. Push yourself and your kids to do more, to do better than you and they have done before. Seek your best educational self, and you'll be amazed at the results.

Appendix

Additional Resources

The tools and resources available in support of your efforts are drawn from the business, outdoor education, and progressive education communities.

- The School Reform Initiative (http://schoolreforminitiative.org/) offers a wide variety of protocols that can be useful for instruction and reflection. Visit the website for a complete listing as well as downloadable instructions.

- Visit the Teacher Tools section of the Critical Skills Program website (http://antiochne.edu/acsr/teachertools/) for an ever-growing catalog of free tools for facilitation, instruction, and debriefing.

Depending on your specific needs and goals, you may wish to explore the following:

Organizations

American Youth Foundation (http://www.ayf.com/)

Antioch University–New England (http://www.antiochne.edu/)

Association for Experiential Education (http://www.aee.org/)

Coalition of Essential Schools (http://www.essentialschools.org/)

Partnership for 21st Century Skills (http://www.p21.org/)

Q.E.D. Foundation (http://www.qedfoundation.org/)

School Reform Initiative (http://www.schoolreforminitiative.org/)

Resources on Facilitation

Bens, Ingrid M. (2012). *Facilitation at a glance! Your pocket guide to facilitation* (3rd ed.). Salem, NH: Goal/QPC.

Schwarz, Roger, Davidson, Anne, Carlson, Peg, & McKinney, Sue, et al. (2005). *Skilled facilitator fieldbook: Tips, tools, and tested methods for consultants, facilitators, managers, trainers, and coaches.* San Francisco, CA: Jossey-Bass.

Wilkinson, Michael. (2004). *The secrets of facilitation: The S.M.A.R.T. guide to getting results with groups.* San Francisco, CA: Jossey-Bass.

Resources on Community Building

Daresh, John C. (with Lynch, Jane). (2010). *Improve learning by building community: A principal's guide to action.* Thousand Oaks, CA: Corwin.

Evanski, Jerry. (2009). *Classroom activators: More than 100 ways to energize learners* (2nd ed.). Thousand Oaks, CA: Corwin.

Frank, Laurie S. (2004). *Journey toward the caring classroom: Using adventure to create community in the classroom.* Oklahoma City, OK: Wood 'N' Barnes.

Johnson, LouAnne. (2011). *Teaching outside the box: How to grab your students by their brains* (2nd ed.). San Francisco, CA: Jossey-Bass.

Kryza, Kathleen, Duncan, Alicia, & Stephens, S. Joy. (2009). *Inspiring elementary learners: Nurturing the whole child in a differentiated classroom.* Thousand Oaks, CA: Corwin.

Springer, Steve, & Alexander, Brandy. (2005). *The organized teacher: A hands-on guide to setting up and running a terrific classroom.* New York, NY: McGraw-Hill.

Thomas, Laura. (2010). *Cooperation isn't enough.* Available from Antioch University–New England, 40 Avon Street, Keene, NH 03431–3516.

Udvari-Solner, Alice, & Kluth, Paula. (2008). *Joyful learning: Active and collaborative learning in inclusive classrooms.* Thousand Oaks, CA: Corwin.

Texts That Outline Philosophies Requiring Next Generation Instruction Skills for Implementation

Dewey, John. (1938). *Experience and education.* New York, NY: Macmillan.

Fried, Robert L. (2005). *The game of school: Why we all play it, how it hurts kids,and what it will take to change it.* San Francisco, CA: Jossey-Bass.

Fried, Robert L. (2001). *Passionate teacher: A practical guide* (2nd ed.). Boston, MA: Beacon Press.

Glasser, William. (1998). *The quality school: Managing students without coercion* (Rev. ed.). New York, NY: HarperCollins.

Mathews, Jay, & Hill, Ian. (2005). *Supertest: How the International Baccalaureate can strengthen our schools.* Peru, IL: Open Court/Carus.

Meier, Deborah. (2002). *The power of their ideas: Lessons for America from a small school in Harlem* (Rev. ed.). Boston, MA: Beacon Press.

Sizer, Theodore R. (2004). *Horace's compromise: The dilemma of the American high school.* New York, NY: Houghton Mifflin. (Originally published 1984)

Sizer, Theodore R., & Faust Sizer, Nancy. (1999). *The students are watching: Schools and the moral contract.* Boston, MA: Beacon Press.

Sobel, David. (2005). *Place-based education: Connecting classrooms & communities* (2nd ed.). Great Barrington, MA: Orion Society.

Wagner, Tony. (2008). *The global achievement gap: Why even our best schools don't teach the new survival skills our children need—and what we can do about it.* New York, NY: Basic Books.

References

Ainsworth, L., & Viegut, D. (2006). *Common formative assessments: How to connect standards-based instruction and assessment.* Thousand Oaks, CA: Corwin.

American Youth Foundation. (1997). *Camp Merrowvista leadership training manual.* St. Louis, MO: American Youth Foundation.

Cairn, R. W., & Coble, T. L. (1993). *Learning by giving: K–8 service-learning curriculum guide.* St. Paul, MN: National Youth Leadership Council.

Carter, K., & QED Assessment Moderation Team. (2011). *Q.E.D. Foundation: Choices for learning, choices for life.* Retrieved from http://www.qedfoundation .org/ (no longer available online)

CCSSO (Common Core State Standards Initiative). (2011). Frequently asked questions. Retrieved from http://www.corestandards.org/frequently-asked-questions/

Corrie, C. (2003). *Becoming emotionally intelligent.* Stafford, UK: Network Educational Press.

Danielson, C. (2010, May). Presentation to the New Hampshire Staff Development Council, Manchester, NH.

Darling-Hammond, L., & McCloskey, L. (2008). Assessment for learning around the world: What would it mean to be "internationally competitive"? *Phi Delta Kappan, 90*(4), 263–272.

Deal, T. E., & Kennedy, A. A. (1983). Culture: A new look through old lenses. *The Journal of Applied Behavioral Science, 19,* 498–505.

Dewey, J. (1916). *Democracy and education.* New York, NY: Macmillan.

Dewey, J. (1938). *Experience and education.* New York, NY: Macmillan.

Facilitator. (2009). In *Encarta World English Dictionary* (North American Edition). Redmond, WA: Microsoft (with Bloomsbury). Retrieved from http://www .bing.com/Dictionary/

Frank, L. S. (2004). *Journey toward the caring classroom: Using adventure to create community in the classroom & beyond.* Oklahoma City, OK: Wood 'N' Barnes.

Fried, Robert L. (2005). *The game of school: Why we all play it, how it hurts kids, and what it will take to change it.* San Francisco, CA: Jossey-Bass.

Fullan, M. (2007). *Leading in a culture of change: Personal action guide and workbook.* San Francisco, CA: Jossey-Bass.

Jacobs, G. M., Power, M. A., & Loh, W. I. (2002). *The teacher's sourcebook for cooperative learning: Practical techniques, basic principles, and frequently asked questions.* Thousand Oaks, CA: Corwin.

Kay, K. (2010). 21st century skills: Why they matter, what they are, and how we get there. In J. A. Bellanca & R. S. Brandt (Eds.), *21st century skills: Rethinking how students learn* (pp. xiii–xxxi). Bloomington, IN: Solution Tree Press.

Kolb, D. A. (1984). *Experiential learning: Experience as the source of learning and development.* Englewood Cliffs, NJ: Prentice Hall.

Maslow. A. H. (1943). A theory of human motivation. *Psychological Review, 50,* 370–396.

McGrath, W. (2001). *Critical skills level I coaching kit.* Keene, NH: Antioch University–New England.

McGrath, W. (2007). *Critical skills level I coaching kit.* Keene, NH: Antioch University–New England.

Meier, D. (2000, February/March). Educating a democracy: Standards and the future of public education. *Boston Review.* Retrieved from http://bostonreview.net/BR24.6/meier.html

National School Reform Faculty. (n.d.). *Zones of comfort, risk and danger: Constructing your zone map.* Retrieved from http://www.nsrfharmony.org/protocol/doc/zones_of_comfort.pdf.

Palmer, P. J. (1987). Community, conflict, and ways of knowing: Ways to deepen our educational agenda. *Change, 19*(5), 20–25.

Posnick-Goodwin, S. (2010). How will the new Common Core State Standards impact teachers? *California Educator, 15*(3). Retrieved from http://www.cta.org/en/Professional-Development/Publications/2010/11/Educator-November-10/Common-core-standards.aspx

Quinn, J. (n.d.). *Quinn's six questions.* Retrieved from http://www.nsrfharmony.org/protocol/doc/quinns_six.pdf

Senge, P. M. (with Cambron-McCabe, N., Lucas, T., Smith, B., Dutton, J., & Kleiner, A.). (2000). *Schools that learn: A fifth discipline fieldbook for educators, parents, and everyone who cares about education.* New York, NY: Doubleday.

Sizer, T. R. (2004). *Horace's compromise: The dilemma of the American high school.* New York, NY: Houghton Mifflin. (Originally published 1984)

Thompson-Grove, G., Frazer, E., & Dunne, F. (further revised by Frazer, E.). (2006). *Pocket guide to probing questions.* Retrieved from http://www.nsrfharmony.org/protocol/doc/probing_questions_guide.pdf

University of Minnesota, Community Service-Learning Center. (2011). Reflection in service-learning classes. Retrieved from http://www.servicelearning.umn.edu/info/reflection.html

Wagner, T. (2008). *The global achievement gap: Why even our best schools don't teach the survival skills our children need—and what we can do about it.* New York, NY: Basic Books.

Wheatley, M. J., & Kellner-Rogers, M. (1996). *A simpler way.* San Francisco, CA: Berrett-Koehler.

Index

Academic Learner Expectations (ALEs), 13
Academic Support handout, 43, 44–45*f*
Aiming phase, 48–55
    assessment, 105, 108–109
    clarity element, 51, 64–65
    cooperative learning, 54
    Framework for Next Generation
        Instruction, 50*f*, 136*f*
    Internet websites, 49
    Next Generation facilitators, 51–54
    Next Generation instruction, 48–49
    probing questions, 51
    student roles, 54–55
American Youth Foundation,
    23, 73–74, 100
    website, 138
Antioch University (New England):
    Center for School Renewal, 8
    Critical Skills Program, 4, 8, 14, 22–23,
        25–26, 49, 138
    website, 49, 138
"Ask three and then me" approach, 74
Assessment:
    Aiming phase, 105, 108–109
    assessment for learning, 104
    assessment of learning, 104
    Challenge Feedback, 122–123*f*
    Claiming phase, 78, 79, 86, 88, 105,
        108–109
    class expectations, 105–106, 113
    Collaboration Checklist, 119–121*f*
    criterion referenced assessment, 104
    defined, 104
    Effort and Participation Rubric, 125–126*f*
    End-of-Day Sheet, 86, 108, 109*f*
    feedback, 104, 105–106, 113*f*
    formative assessment, 104
    Framing phase, 105
    Full-Value Contract, 113

Gaming phase, 105
Great Aunt Mildred's Space Shot
    Rubric, 128–130*f*
Great Aunt Mildred's U.S. Tour Rubric,
    131–134*f*
instructional bias, 104
Leadership Checklist, 114–115*f*
Next Generation facilitators,
    105, 106–108, 112, 134
norm referenced assessment, 104
Oral Communications Rubric, 123–124*f*
Organization Checklist, 116–117*f*
probing questions, 106–108
Product Quality Checklist, 121–122*f*
purpose of, 104
quality criteria, 108–112
Science Progress Report Example,
    127–128*f*
Self-Direction Checklist, 118–119*f*
summative assessment, 104, 107, 108
traditional approach, 103–104, 105
Assessment for learning, 104
Assessment of learning, 104
Association for Experiential
    Education, 138
Autopsy technique, 90

Ball of String, 100
Base Teams Challenge, 42, 43*f*
Blogs, 86
Buck Institute for Education, 49

Callahan, Dan (Pine Glen Elementary
    School, Massachusetts):
    Aiming phase, 53–54
    collaborative learning community
        (CLC), 35
    Framing phase, 61–62
    Gaming phase, 74

instructional profile, 15–16
Next Generation instruction, 20
technology integration, 15–16, 20, 35,
    53–54, 61–62
Carousel, 41–42
Carter, Kim, 91
Chalk talk, 87
Challenge Feedback, 122–123*f*
Chunking strategy, 56–57, 59
Claiming phase, 77–94
    assessment, 78, 79, 86, 88, 105, 108–109
    class expectations, 90
    communication loop, 87
    concrete recall, 83, 84, 86
    debriefing session, 78–79
    evaluation of effort, 83, 84, 86, 88
    facilitation activities, 99–102
    facilitation techniques, 97–99
    feedback, 87–88
    Framework for Next Generation
        Instruction, 78*f*, 136*f*
    Next Generation facilitators, 78–79, 85,
        86–87, 89–91
    probing questions, 79, 83, 88
    reflection process, 77–78, 84
    reflection rubrics, 83*f*, 91–94*f*
    reflection tools, 85–87, 88, 89–90
    SPIN-on-learning technique,
        79, 80*f*, 81*f*, 82*f*
    technology integration, 79
    transfer of learning, 83, 84, 85, 86, 89
Clarity element:
    Aiming phase, 51, 64–65
    Framing phase, 63–65
    Gaming phase, 71–73
Class expectations:
    assessment, 105–106, 113
    Claiming phase, 90
    collaborative learning community
        (CLC), 40–45
    facilitation techniques, 98
    Framing phase, 56–57
Classroom culture, 27
Classroom Policies, 42–43*f*
Coalition of Essential Schools
    (CES), 4, 12, 18
    website, 49, 138
Cocktail-party phase, 35
Collaboration Checklist, 119–121*f*
Collaborative activities:
    I Like People Who, 45
    Last Name Lineup, 46
    Liars' Club, 46

Line Up, 46
Partner Introductions, 46
People to People, 46
Personality Bingo, 45
Pinwheels, 46
Scavenger Hunt, 45
Speed Grouping, 46
Two Truths and a Lie, 46
Collaborative learning community
    (CLC), 25–47
    Academic Support handout, 43, 44–45*f*
    Base Teams Challenge, 42, 43*f*
    class expectations, 40–45
    classroom creation, 32–47
    classroom culture, 27
    Classroom Policies, 42–43*f*
    classroom profile, 28–30
    cocktail-party phase, 35
    Collaboration stage, 31–32, 47
    Cooperation stage, 31, 32–47
    Critical Skills Model of Instruction,
        30–47
    defined, 25–27
    Framework for Next Generation
        Instruction, 23–24, 26*f*, 136*f*
    Full-Value Contract, 40, 41
    Give to Get process, 41–42
    hierarchy of needs, 27–28
    individual member contributions, 27
    Knowledge/Communication stage,
        30–31, 32–47
    Maturation/Maintenance stage, 32, 47
    Next Generation facilitators, 28–29,
        33–35, 39–40, 41–45
    purposefully structured/actively
        maintained, 26–27
    risk-taking zones, 36–37, 38*f*
    teacher/student full membership, 27
    team-building activities, 45–47
    Trust stage, 31, 32–47
Common Core State Standards, 19, 23
Communication loop, 87
Compass Points, 101–102
Concentric Circles, 100
Constructivist methods, 2, 19
Cooperative learning, 54
Criterion referenced assessment, 104
Critical Skills Level I Coaching Kit, 65
Critical Skills Model of Instruction:
    Collaboration stage, 31–32, 47
    collaborative learning community
        (CLC), 30–47
    Cooperation stage, 31, 32–47

Knowledge/Communication stage,
  30–31, 32–47
Maturation/Maintenance stage, 32, 47
Trust stage, 31, 32–47

Danielson, Charlotte, 75
Debriefing session:
  Claiming phase, 78–79
  Gaming phase, 68, 71
Dunham, Beth, 11
Dyads, 100

"Eat a Bit-O-Honey" technique, 73–74
Effort and Participation Rubric, 125–126*f*
Emotion Cards, 100
End-of-Day Sheet, 86, 108, 109*f*
Exclaiming phase, 94–96
  celebration activities, 94–95
  facilitation activities, 99–102
  facilitation techniques, 97–99
  Framework for Next Generation
    Instruction, 95*f*, 136*f*
  Next Generation facilitators, 95–96
Exit slips, 86, 87, 88, 90
Experiential learning, 2, 21–23, 58

Feedback:
  assessment, 104, 105–106, 113*f*
  Claiming phase, 87–88
  giving-feedback guidelines, 113*f*
  receiving-feedback guidelines, 113*f*
Fish Bowling, 100
Fist to Five, 86, 100
Ford Motor Company Challenge, 65–67
Formative assessment, 104
Found Objects, 100
Framework for Next Generation
    Instruction:
  Aiming phase, 50*f*, 136*f*
  Claiming phase, 78*f*, 136*f*
  collaborative learning community
    (CLC), 23–24, 26*f*, 136*f*
  completed model, 136*f*
  Exclaiming phase, 95*f*, 136*f*
  Framing phase, 57*f*, 136*f*
  Gaming phase, 68*f*, 136*f*
  model template, 24*f*
Framing phase, 56–67
  assessment, 105
  chunking strategy, 56–57, 59
  clarity element, 63–65
  class expectations, 56–57
  experiential learning, 58

Ford Motor Company Challenge, 65–67
Framework for Next Generation
    Instruction, 57*f*, 136*f*
frontloading, 58
Full-Value Contract, 56–57
Great Aunt Mildred challenge, 60–61, 63
instructional "sweet spot," 62
Next Generation facilitators, 58–67
probing questions, 57, 62
Religion Poster activity, 64
scaffolding, 63
technology integration, 61–62
Frontloading, 58
Full-Value Contract:
  assessment, 113
  collaborative learning community
    (CLC), 40, 41
  facilitation techniques, 98
  Framing phase, 56–57

Gaming phase, 67–76
  assessment, 105
  clarity element, 71–73
  debriefing session, 68, 71
  "Eat a Bit-O-Honey" technique, 73–74
  facilitation activities, 99–102
  facilitation techniques, 97–99
  Framework for Next Generation
    Instruction, 68*f*, 136*f*
  Next Generation facilitators, 68–69,
    70–72, 73–74
  probing questions, 68, 70, 73, 74, 75
  student roles, 74
Gardner, Howard, 53
George Lucas Educational Foundation/
    Edutopia, 49
Give to Get process, 41–42
Great Aunt Mildred challenge:
  scaffolding, 63
  Space Shot, 61
  Space Shot Rubric, 128–130*f*
  U.S. Tour, 60–61
  U.S. Tour Rubric, 131–134*f*

Hart, Maura, 41–42
Haunting of Hill House, The (Jackson),
    107–108
Hierarchy of needs, 27–28
Hodson, Louise Van Order
    (Compass School, Vermont):
  Aiming phase, 53
  collaborative learning community
    (CLC), 40

Exclaiming phase, 96
Framing phase, 61
Gaming phase, 72
instructional profile, 11
Huard, Jenn (Souhegan High School,
    New Hampshire):
  Academic Learner Expectations
    (ALEs), 13
  Academic Support handout, 43, 44–45f
  Aiming phase, 53
  assessment, 106, 125–126f
  Claiming phase, 78–79, 87, 90–91
  collaborative learning community
    (CLC), 33–34, 40, 43, 44–45f
  Exclaiming phase, 96
  Framing phase, 59–60
  Gaming phase, 71–72
  instructional profile, 11–13
  Mission Statement, 90
  S-M-A-R-T-E-R method, 53
  Souhegan Six Behavioral
    Expectations, 90
  Understanding by Design, 53
Hunter, Erin (River Valley Technical
    Center, Vermont):
  Aiming phase, 51–52
  assessment, 134
  Claiming phase, 89
  collaborative learning community
    (CLC), 28–29, 34, 41–42
  Gaming phase, 70–71, 73
  Give to Get process, 41–42
  instructional profile, 6–7

I Like People Who, 45
Inquiry-driven instruction, 2, 19, 23
International Baccalaureate, 23, 49
Internet websites:
  Aiming phase, 49
  American Youth Foundation, 138
  Association for Experiential
    Education, 138
  Buck Institute for Education, 49
  Coalition of Essential Schools (CES),
    49, 138
  Critical Skills Program (Antioch
    University), 49, 138
  George Lucas Educational Foundation/
    Edutopia, 49
  International Baccalaureate, 49
  National School Reform Initiative, 138
  National Service-Learning
    Clearinghouse, 49

Partnership for 21st Century
    Skills, 138
  QED Foundation, 49, 138
  Religion Poster activity, 64

Jackson, Shirley, 107–108
Jacobs, G. M., 55
Journaling, 86, 101

Phi Delta Kappan, 18
Kohn, Alfie, 15
KWLs, 87

Last Name Lineup, 46
Leadership Checklist, 114–115f
Learning logs, 86
Lemieux, Chris (Otter Valley Union
    High School, Vermont):
  Aiming phase, 52–53
  assessment, 112, 121–124f, 127–128f
  Claiming phase, 85
  collaborative learning community
    (CLC), 34–35
  Exclaiming phase, 95–96
  Framing phase, 59
  instructional profile, 9–11
Letter to Self, 101
Liars' Club, 46
Lifelong Learner, 89
Line Up, 46
Loh, W. I., 55

Magnusson, Al (Hampton Academy,
    New Hampshire):
  assessment, 112, 127–128f
  Claiming phase, 79, 86–87
  collaborative learning community
    (CLC), 39–40
  Ford Motor Company challenge, 65–67
  Framing phase, 58–59, 62, 65–67
  Gaming phase, 68, 69, 70, 71
  instructional profile, 4–6
  SPIN-on-learning technique,
    79, 80f, 81f, 82f
Mapping, 101
Maslow, Abraham, 27
Mission Statement, 90
Multiple intelligences, 53

National School Reform Initiative:
  probing questions, 75
  risk-taking zones, 36–37, 38f
  website, 138

National Service-Learning
    Clearinghouse, 49
New pedagogy, 1–3
    constructivist methods, 2, 19
    facilitation, 3
    facilitators, 3
    learning presuppositions, 2
    Next Generation instruction, 18–21
Next Generation facilitators, 4–16
    Aiming phase, 51–54
    assessment, 105, 106–108, 112, 134
    Claiming phase, 78–79, 85, 86–87,
        89–91
    collaborative learning community
        (CLC), 28–29, 33–35, 39–40, 41–45
    Exclaiming phase, 95–96
    Framing phase, 58–67
    Gaming phase, 68–69, 70–72, 73–74
    See also specific instructor
Next Generation instruction:
    Aiming phase, 48–49
    critical skills model, 22–23
    defined, 18
    experiential learning, 21–23
    facilitation activities, 99–102
    facilitation techniques, 97–99
    Framework for Next Generation
        Instruction, 23, 24f
    instructional transition, 135–137
    new pedagogy, 18–21
    purpose of, 21–24
    teaching image, 17
    technology integration, 20
Next Generation instruction activities,
    99–102
    Ball of String, 100
    Compass Points, 101–102
    Concentric Circles, 100
    Dyads, 100
    Emotion Cards, 100
    Fish Bowling, 100
    Fist to Five, 86, 100
    Found Objects, 100
    Journaling, 86, 101
    Letter to Self, 101
    Mapping, 101
    North-South-East-West, 101–102
    One-Word Whip, 100
    Postcards, 100
    Shared Learning Circle, 101
    Skills List, 100
    Spider Web, 100
    Triads, 100

Next Generation instruction techniques,
    97–99
Norm referenced assessment, 104
North-South-East-West, 101–102

One-Word Whip, 100
Oral Communications Rubric, 123–124f
Organization Checklist, 116–117f

Partner Introductions, 46
Partnership for 21st Century Skills, 18, 138
Pathwise (Danielson), 75
People to People, 46
Perlow, Bruce (Otter Valley Union High
    School, Vermont):
    Aiming phase, 52–53
    assessment, 112, 121–124f, 127–128f
    Claiming phase, 85
    collaborative learning community
        (CLC), 34–35
    Exclaiming phase, 95–96
    Framing phase, 59
    instructional profile, 8–9
Personality Bingo, 45
Pinwheels, 46
Place-based education, 2, 23
Place-based learning, 19
Postcards, 100
Power, M. A., 55
Problem-based learning, 2, 19, 23
Product Quality Checklist, 121–122f
Progress reports, 87, 127–128f
Project-based learning, 2, 19, 23
Punished by Rewards (Kohn), 15

QED Foundation:
    reflection rubric, 83f, 91
    website, 49, 138
Quality criteria:
    assessment tools, 112, 114–134
    content criteria, 111
    development procedure, 110–112
    form criteria, 111
    in assessment, 108–112
    process criteria, 111

Reflection process:
    defined, 77–78, 84
    rubrics, 83f, 91–94f
    tools, 85–87, 88, 89–90
    See also Claiming phase
Religion Poster activity, 63–64
Report cards, 87

Resources:
  Next Generation instructional skills,
      139–140
  on community building, 139
  on facilitation, 138–139
  organizations, 138
  See also Internet websites
Risk-taking zones:
  collaborative learning community
      (CLC), 36–37, 38*f*
  comfort zone, 36
  danger zone, 37
  risk zone, 37
  student differences, 37, 38*f*
Robinson, Allison (Monadnock Regional
    Middle/High School, New
    Hampshire):
  Aiming phase, 53
  assessment, 112, 128–130*f*, 131–134*f*
  Autopsy technique, 90
  Base Teams Challenge, 42, 43*f*
  Claiming phase, 90
  Classroom Policies, 42–43*f*
  collaborative learning community
      (CLC), 42–43
  Framing phase, 59, 60–61, 63–64
  Gaming phase, 68
  Great Aunt Mildred challenge, 60–61,
      63, 128–130*f*, 131–134*f*
  instructional profile, 13–15
  Religion Poster activity, 63–64
Romeo and Juliet, 76

Scaffolding, 63
Scavenger Hunt, 45
Science Progress Report Example,
    127–128*f*
Self-Direction Checklist, 118–119*f*
Service learning, 2, 19, 23
Shared Learning Circle, 101
Skills List, 100
Skype, 62
S-M-A-R-T-E-R method, 53

Speed Grouping, 46
Spider Web, 100
SPIN-on-learning technique:
  biology rubric, 82*f*
  chemistry rubric, 81*f*
  description of, 79
  physical science rubric, 80*f*
Steele, Caitlin (Otter Valley Union High
    School, Vermont):
  Aiming phase, 52–53
  assessment, 112, 121–124*f*, 127–128*f*
  Claiming phase, 85
  collaborative learning community
      (CLC), 29, 34–35
  Exclaiming phase, 95–96
  Framing phase, 59
  instructional profile, 7–8
Student roles:
  Aiming phase, 54–55
  Gaming phase, 74
Summative assessment, 104, 107, 108

T charts, 89
*Teacher's Sourcebook for Cooperative
    Learning, The* (Jacobs, Power, and
    Loh), 55
Technology integration:
  Aiming phase, 53–54
  Claiming phase, 79
  collaborative learning community
      (CLC), 35
  Framing phase, 61–62
  Next Generation facilitator, 15–16
  Next Generation instruction, 20
Think/Pair/Share, 41–42
Triads, 100
21st century skills, 18
Twitter, 86, 88
Two Truths and a Lie, 46

Understanding by Design, 53

Vorsteg, Anna Kay, 73–74

CORWIN
A SAGE Company

The Corwin logo—a raven striding across an open book—represents the union of courage and learning. Corwin is committed to improving education for all learners by publishing books and other professional development resources for those serving the field of PreK–12 education. By providing practical, hands-on materials, Corwin continues to carry out the promise of its motto: **"Helping Educators Do Their Work Better."**